Assessing the Costs and Benefits of LifeSet

The Youth Villages Program Model for Transition-Age Youth

LYNN A. KAROLY

RAND SOCIAL AND ECONOMIC WELL-BEING

Sponsored by Youth Villages

For more information on this publication, visit www.rand.org/t/RR2839

Library of Congress Cataloging-in-Publication Data is available for this publication.

ISBN: 978-1-9774-0438-1

Published by the RAND Corporation, Santa Monica, Calif.

Cover: Geber86 / Getty Images.

Preface

LifeSet, operated by Youth Villages (formerly known as YVLifeSet), is a program that serves young adults, ages 17 to 22, who are aging out of the foster care system. Through intensive case management and other services, LifeSet seeks to ensure a successful transition to adulthood for these vulnerable young adults, with a particular focus on accessing and maintaining stable and suitable housing, remaining free from contact with the criminal justice system, participating in further education and vocational training, obtaining and maintaining employment, and developing other skills required for responsible adulthood. LifeSet has been evaluated using an experimental design conducted in Tennessee in the early 2010s and found to improve earnings, housing stability, economic well-being, health, safety, and criminal involvement.

The goal of this study is to conduct a rigorous analysis of the costs and benefits of LifeSet, integrating the best available research evidence on the economic values of the outcomes affected by the program. The resulting analysis of benefits and costs will inform decisionmakers at Youth Villages and elsewhere regarding the potential for a positive economic return from investing in the LifeSet model.

This study was sponsored by Youth Villages. It will be of interest to those associated with the LifeSet program, as well as those interested more generally in the costs and benefits of programs serving young adults transitioning out of the foster care system.

RAND Social and Economic Well-Being is a division of the RAND Corporation that seeks to actively improve the health and social and economic well-being of populations and communities throughout the world. This research was conducted in the Social and Behavioral Policy Program within RAND Social and Economic Well-Being. The program focuses on such topics as risk factors and prevention programs, social safety net programs and other social supports, poverty, aging, disability, child and youth health and well-being, and quality of life, as well as other policy concerns that are influenced by social and behavioral actions and systems that affect well-being. For more information, email sbp@rand.org.

Contents

Preface ... iii
Figure ... vi
Tables ... vii
Summary ... viii
Acknowledgments ... xiii
Abbreviations ... xiv

1. Introduction ... 1
   Study Objective and Approach ... 3
   Road Map for the Report ... 4
2. Evidence of Cost and Outcomes for LifeSet ... 5
   Estimated Total Cost of LifeSet in the MDRC Evaluation ... 6
   Estimated Impacts of LifeSet in the MDRC Evaluation ... 6
3. Valuing the Outcomes from LifeSet ... 11
   Education and Training ... 11
   Employment and Earnings ... 15
   Housing Stability ... 15
   Economic Well-Being ... 16
   Health ... 17
   Safety ... 18
   Social Support ... 18
   Criminal Involvement ... 19
4. Comprehensive Benefit-Cost Analysis for LifeSet ... 21
   Cost of LifeSet ... 21
   Benefits (and Costs) from the Estimated Impacts of LifeSet ... 21
   Estimated Net Benefits of LifeSet ... 23
   Accounting for Uncertainty in the Included Impacts ... 24
   Potential Unmeasured Benefits (and Costs) of LifeSet ... 24
   Comparison of Retrospective BCA with WSIPP Prospective BCA ... 26
5. Conclusions and Implications ... 27
   Key Findings ... 27
   Implications ... 29

Appendix A. Methods and Findings from the WSIPP BCA of LifeSet 33
Appendix B. Impact Estimates from Evaluation of LifeSet 40
Appendix C. Adjustment to Program Cost 46
Appendix D. Monte Carlo Simulation Analysis 50

References 53

Figure

Figure 1.1. LifeSet Logic Model.......... 2

Tables

Table S.1. Summary of the Estimated Cost and Benefits of LifeSet per Participant Under Alternative Assumptions, 2015 Dollars x
Table 2.1. Summary of Estimated Impacts by Domain and Year 7
Table 3.1. Sources of Shadow Values for LifeSet Impacts in MDRC Evaluation 12
Table 3.2. Parameter Assumptions for Public Benefit Programs 17
Table 4.1. Estimated Cost and Benefits of LifeSet per Participant Under Alternative Assumptions, 2015 Dollars 22
Table A.1. LifeSet Impacts in MDRC Evaluation and Those Included in WSIPP BCA 35
Table A.2. WSIPP Effect Sizes Versus MDRC Evaluation 37
Table A.3. WSIPP Model BCA Results 39
Table B.1. One- and Two-Year Impact Estimates: Education and Training 40
Table B.2. One- and Two-Year Impact Estimates: Employment and Earnings 41
Table B.3. One-Year Impact Estimates: Housing Stability 41
Table B.4. One-Year Impact Estimates: Economic Well-Being 42
Table B.5. One-Year Impact Estimates: Health 42
Table B.6. One-Year Impact Estimates: Safety 43
Table B.7. One-Year Impact Estimates: Social Support 44
Table B.8. One- and Two-Year Impact Estimates: Criminal Involvement 45
Table C.1. LifeSet Cost per Participant 46
Table C.2. Service Utilization by Treatment and Control Group Participants 47
Table C.3. Participation in LifeSet Sessions for Treatment Group Participants 48
Table D.1. Parameter Assumptions for Monte Carlo Simulation 51
Table D.2. Monte Carlo Simulation Results 52

Summary

LifeSet (known previously as YVLifeSet), operated by Youth Villages in 14 states and the District of Columbia, provides intensive case management and other services for young adults, ages 17 to 22, aging out of the foster care system. The program was evaluated by MDRC, using an experimental design (i.e., a randomized control trial [RCT]), for a cohort of participants in Tennessee who enrolled in the program between October 2010 and October 2012, with findings reported one year and two years after randomization. Based largely on survey data, the evaluation examined measures after one year in six domains in which the program was expected to have an impact: education and training, employment and earnings, housing stability and economic well-being, health and safety, social support, and criminal involvement. Administrative data available up to two years postenrollment captured outcomes in three of the six domains: education and training, employment and earnings, and criminal involvement. Overall, the evaluation found favorable and statistically significant impacts on at least one primary outcome in three domains: employment and earnings, housing stability and economic well-being, and health and safety. None of the outcomes in the education and training and social support domains was statistically significant. One secondary outcome was favorable and statistically significant in the criminal involvement domain.

Study Objective and Approach

The aim of this study was to conduct a rigorous retrospective analysis of the costs and benefits of LifeSet, as implemented by Youth Villages in Tennessee and evaluated by MDRC. Our approach follows best-practice recommendations for performing benefit-cost analyses (BCAs) offered by a recent National Academy of Sciences panel. We build on the foundation of the MDRC evaluation, to understand both the resources required to implement LifeSet—and therefore program costs—and the impacts of the program on the outcome domains and indicators examined in the two-year MDRC evaluation.

In particular, we relied on estimates of program cost generated by MDRC as part of the RCT evaluation, with an adjustment to account for the use of services by young adults in the control group—i.e., the counterfactual, business as usual. Likewise, we used the estimates of program impact published by MDRC and attached economic values to as many of the outcomes as feasible. In some cases, the economic impacts were projected into the future, beyond the point of last follow-up. Because the impact estimates were not always favorable for the treatment group, the impacts of LifeSet were associated with both positive benefits and negative benefits (or costs). Given uncertainty in the dollar valuation of the outcomes measured in the evaluation, we produced a more conservative estimate of total value of the outcomes and a less conservative estimate, with a base-case estimate that used the midpoint between the two bounds. Our BCA was performed from the societal perspective, and we used a 3 percent discount rate. Monetary amounts are reported in 2015 dollars, the same year as the MDRC cost analysis for the LifeSet evaluation.

In the remainder of this summary, we highlight key findings and discuss the implications of the analysis for understanding the economic returns from LifeSet.

Key Findings

The BCA of LifeSet presented in this report produced the following key findings (see Table S.1):

- LifeSet cost an estimated $8,400 per participant more than "business as usual" in 2015 dollars. The gross cost of LifeSet per participant as implemented in Tennessee was estimated to be about $11,800. Accounting for upper- and lower-bound estimates of the value of services used by young adults in the control group, LifeSet cost an estimated $8,000 to $8,800 per participant more than the control group, with a midpoint base-case estimate of about $8,400 per participant. This is the range of cost estimates that we compare with the value of the impacts generated by the program when determining the economic return.
- **For the observed outcomes that could be valued, LifeSet was estimated to generate present-value net benefits ranging from about $4,100 to $8,900 per participant.** Outcomes were measured for treatment and control group members by a survey administered 12 months after randomization and by administrative data capturing outcomes up to two years after randomization. Most of the benefits from the observed outcomes derive from the estimated reduction in victimization cost associated with the statistically significant impact of LifeSet in reducing intimate partner violence. All other domains of observed impact are associated with small positive or negative benefits (largely because the impact estimates were small and statistically insignificant) that effectively cancel each other out.
- **LifeSet was estimated to produce additional present-value net benefits ranging from about $4,000 to $5,800 per participant from projected future outcomes.** Based on the observed impacts of LifeSet on educational attainment, future benefits in the form of productivity gains (i.e., higher labor market earnings and fringe benefits), as well as nonmarket benefits (e.g., reductions in crime), were estimated and discounted to present-value dollars.
- **If LifeSet is paid for with tax dollars, the net public dollars required would result in economic costs that partially offset the economic benefits.** It is common to account for the distortionary effects of taxes on economic activity (also known as *deadweight cost*) associated with the funds required to pay for a program, net of any increase or decrease in taxes based on the program impacts. A more conservative estimate in the case of LifeSet produced a deadweight cost of about $4,400 per participant, while a less conservative estimate assumed that there was no such deadweight cost (which would arise if the program were paid for by private funds). The midpoint estimate of deadweight costs falls in between, at $2,100.

Table S.1. Summary of the Estimated Cost and Benefits of LifeSet per Participant Under Alternative Assumptions, 2015 Dollars

Summary Result	More Conservative Estimate	Base-Case Estimate	Less Conservative Estimate
Present-value cost net of control group services	**8,763**	**8,357**	**7,951**
Present-value of outcomes and deadweight cost	**3,708**	**9,338**	**14,706**
Present-value benefits	8,077	11,391	14,706
From observed outcomes	4,101	6,506	8,912
From projected outcomes	3,976	4,885	5,794
Deadweight cost	–4,368	–2,053	0
Present-value net benefits	**–5,055**	**981**	**6,755**
Outcomes not valued			
Vocational education cost, productivity gain, and other benefits	?	?	?
Nonpecuniary cost of housing insecurity	+	+	+
Nonpecuniary cost of economic insecurity	+	+	+
Mental health problems	+	+	+
Health status, insurance coverage, and care utilization	?	?	?
Use of illegal drugs	+	+	+
Use of condoms	+	+	+
Nonpecuniary value of social support	+	+	+
Cost of carrying a handgun	+	+	+

NOTES: A plus sign indicates that expected present-value net benefits would be positive, based on the estimated impact. A question mark indicates that the expected present-value net benefits may be positive or negative given possible countervailing effects.

- **In sum, LifeSet results in estimated present-value net benefits per participant ranging from –$5,100 to $6,800, with a base-case estimate of about $1,000 per participant.** The midpoint estimate and the bottom line for the range of net benefits account for program cost, net benefits from observed and projected outcomes, and deadweight cost. Under the more conservative assumptions, the value of observed and projected benefits is almost sufficient to cover the cost of the program. The assumed deadweight cost accounted for almost all of the estimated negative net benefits. The estimated positive net benefits under the less conservative assumptions resulted from assuming higher economic values for the affected outcomes and from assuming no deadweight cost.
- **The benefit-cost ratio exceeds 1.00 for the base case and less conservative assumptions.** Using the less conservative estimate of present-value net benefits resulted in an estimated benefit-cost ratio of about 1.85, nearly $2 in benefits for every dollar of cost. This can be viewed as a likely upper bound of the economic returns from LifeSet, as implemented and evaluated in Tennessee. The midpoint estimate indicated a favorable benefit-cost ratio of 1.10, whereas the ratio is less than 1.00 (0.42) under the more conservative assumptions, indicating that costs exceed benefits.

- **Accounting for uncertainty in the impacts and economic values of the included outcomes, present-value net benefits are positive 53 percent of the time.** In addition to estimating the lower bound (more conservative) and the upper bound (less conservative) of the net benefits, we also performed a Monte Carlo simulation analysis, which accounted for uncertainty in both impact estimates and the economic values of the outcomes that could be included in the analysis. In just over one-half of the simulations, present-value net benefits exceeded zero, indicating a positive economic return.
- **If all outcomes could be valued, the estimated net benefits from LifeSet are likely to be even larger.** As is often the case with social programs, it was not possible to generate an economic value of all of the outcomes examined in the LifeSet RCT. For most of the omitted outcomes (see Table S.1), the direction of the estimated impacts of LifeSet would be expected to produce additional net benefits to society. In the case of the impacts on vocational education and health-related outcomes, the net benefits could be positive, negative, or zero, because there would be increases in both costs and benefits. The overall contribution of these omitted outcomes is therefore uncertain, although likely to be positive if vocational education and investments in health produce positive net benefits in the long run. Nevertheless, because the magnitudes of the impacts on the outcomes that are not valued were typically small and statistically insignificant, these omitted sources of potential benefits are not likely to generate net benefits that are substantially larger than those already included in the estimate.

Implications

As a retrospective analysis, the BCA of LifeSet presented in this report is a guide to the likely costs and benefits of implementing the program under current conditions in Tennessee and in other jurisdictions in the United States. However, the estimated economic return for Tennessee is not a guarantee of what would be realized in other settings. Any prospective analysis of the costs and benefits of implementing LifeSet under current conditions in a given jurisdiction would need to carefully consider the likely cost of implementing the model with fidelity in that setting, the characteristics and current (baseline) outcomes of the population to be served, and the availability and effectiveness of the existing services available to the target group of young adults in the community of interest. There are reasons to expect that returns could be higher, since LifeSet might have become more efficient to deliver over time, with a lower cost per participant, and it might have become more effective over time because of improved practice. But returns could also be lower if programs serve a less vulnerable population of young adults or if communities have existing programs serving the targeted young adults that are equally cost-effective.

As Youth Villages seeks to improve implementation of LifeSet and disseminate the model to other communities, future RCTs would determine whether the results from the Tennessee evaluation can be generalized to other settings. This analysis suggests several steps that Youth Villages can take in future evaluations to strengthen the evidence regarding the program's economic benefits, in particular. These include the following:

- Collect comprehensive information about the cost of program implementation for both the services provided to LifeSet participants and the "business as usual" services taken up by the control group. This insight into the cost of implementation will support the accurate estimation of the incremental cost of LifeSet relative to the status quo.
- Measure all relevant outcomes that may be affected by the intervention, especially those that can produce public savings and private benefits. Furthermore, go beyond measuring the incidence of any given outcome to also capture the associated magnitude (or quantity) of the impact (e.g., postsecondary education credits earned, not just enrollment). Capturing outcomes in more detail will support more-precise estimation of the economic value of the impacts of LifeSet.
- Where possible, extend the measurement of outcomes beyond the end of the intervention to capture longer-term impacts. Reliance on administrative data can support longer-term measurement, but it is also important to survey treatment and control group members periodically to measure longer-term outcomes that are not captured by administrative data sources.

Youth Villages has demonstrated a commitment to evaluating the impacts of LifeSet and its other programs serving children and young adults in the child welfare system. The addition of economic evaluation—and BCA, in particular—further strengthens our understanding of the resources required for program implementation, as well as the potential for economic benefits to program participants and the rest of the society (as taxpayers and as private citizens) that outweigh the program cost.

Acknowledgments

Sarah Hurley, Youth Villages managing director of data science, provided invaluable guidance throughout the course of this study. Other Youth Villages staff who informed the analyses include Tim Goldsmith, Pat Lawler, Katja Russell, and Walter Meyer. Mark Courtney of the School of Social Service Administration at the University of Chicago and Fred Wulczyn of Chapin Hall at the University of Chicago, both members of the Youth Villages Evaluation and Research Advisory Committee, contributed useful feedback at the study design phase and through comments on the report draft. The research team also benefited from input provided by Jessica Lupo, Woody McCutchen, and Mindy Tarlow of the Edna McConnell Clark Foundation Blue Meridian Partners initiative. Erin Valentine at MDRC graciously provided background information on MDRC's evaluation of LifeSet.

We would also like to acknowledge the thorough technical reviews of the draft report provided by Dana Schultz of RAND and Erin Maher at the University of Oklahoma. At RAND, Thomas Goughnour provided technical support for the analysis.

Abbreviations

BCA	benefit-cost analysis
C	control
CPI	Consumer Price Index
CPS	Current Population Survey
GED	general equivalency diploma
NSC	National Student Clearinghouse
RCT	randomized control trial
SNAP	Supplemental Nutrition Assistance Program
SSI	Supplemental Security Income
T	treatment
TANF	Temporary Assistance for Needy Families
UI	Unemployment Insurance
WIC	Special Supplemental Nutrition Program for Women, Infants, and Children
WSIPP	Washington State Institute for Public Policy

1. Introduction

LifeSet (known previously as YVLifeSet) provides intensive case management and other services for young adults, ages 17 to 22, aging out of the foster care system.[1] Operated by Youth Villages in Tennessee, starting in 1999, and now delivered in multiple communities in 14 states, LifeSet provides supports to ensure a successful transition to adulthood through intensive case management. The program assists with accessing and maintaining stable and suitable housing, remaining free from contact with the criminal justice system, participating in further education and vocational training, engaging in employment, and developing other skills required for responsible adulthood (Youth Villages, undated). The voluntary program provides specially trained LifeSet specialists who meet with participants at least once a week in community settings and are available to provide around-the-clock support for six to nine months, based on the young person's needs.

The LifeSet logic model (Figure 1.1) illustrates how the various practice elements of the model are deployed to achieve the model principles—*systemic assessment*, *safety*, *maximizing outcomes*, *youth driven*, *comprehensive support networks*, *team*, *intensity of engagement*, and *education/vocation*—with the expectation of improving a set of instrumental outcomes. These elements also aim to improve longer-term outcomes related to the young adult's well-being, such as a stable housing situation and improvements in education and training. Other outcomes relate to the retention of quality staff to ensure the delivery of high-quality services.

LifeSet was evaluated using an experimental design by MDRC, with findings reported one year and two years after randomization (Manno et al., 2014; Valentine, Skemer, and Courtney, 2015; Skemer and Valentine, 2016). With both implementation and impact components, the evaluation assigned approximately 1,300 young adults, ages 18 to 24, in Tennessee either to participate in LifeSet or to a control group that received the usual community services. Based largely on survey data, the evaluation examined measures after one year in six domains in which the program was expected to have an impact: education and training, employment and earnings, housing stability and economic well-being, health and safety, social support, and criminal involvement. Administrative data available up to two years postenrollment captured additional outcomes in three of the six domains: education and training, employment and earnings, and criminal involvement.

[1] A growing body of research documents the challenges and adverse outcomes faced by youth transitioning to adulthood from foster care and the juvenile justice system. For a review of prior research and alternative service models, see Manno et al. (2014).

Figure 1.1. LifeSet Logic Model

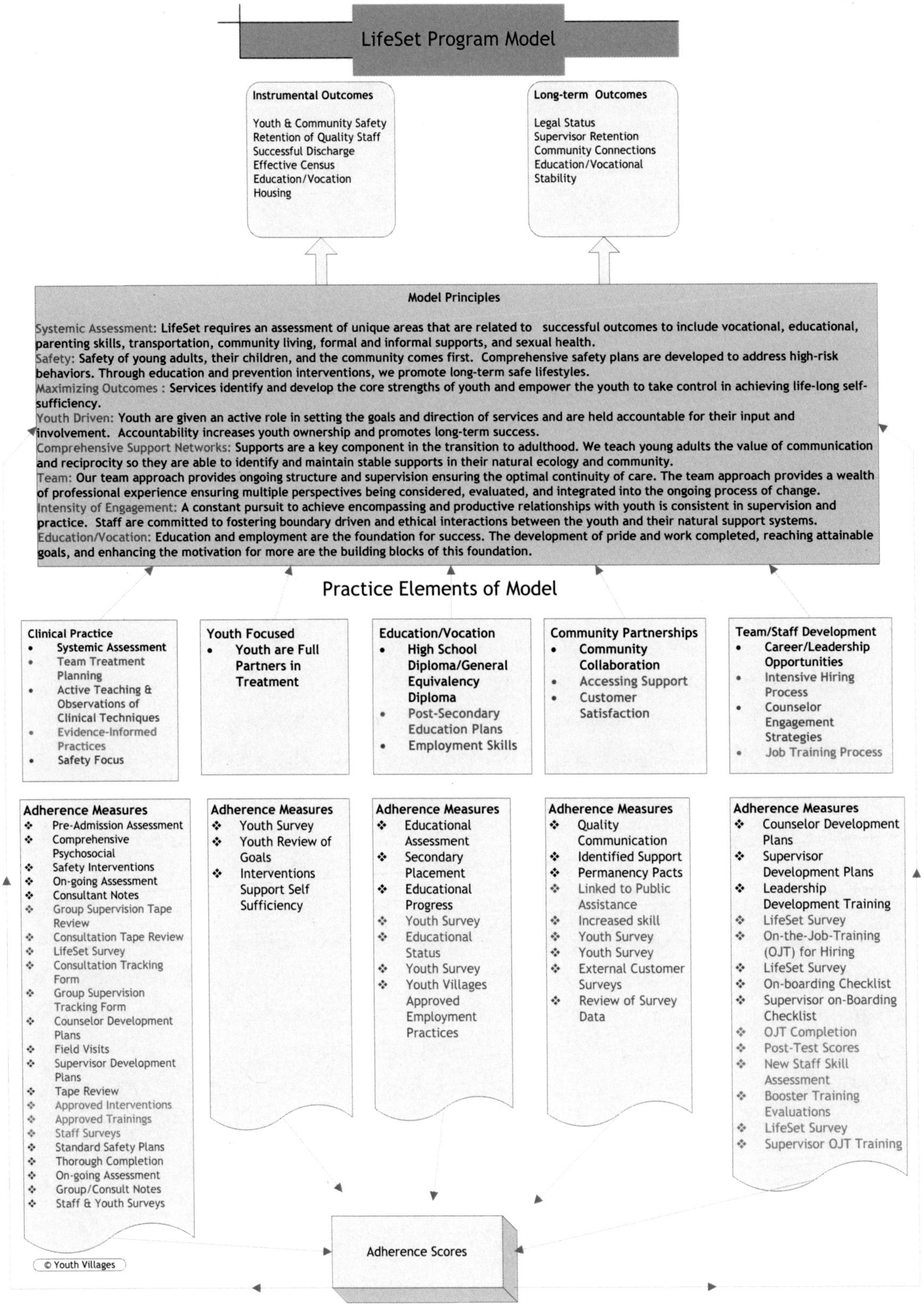

SOURCE: Provided by Youth Villages.

Overall, the evaluation found favorable and statistically significant impacts on at least one primary indicator in three domains: employment and earnings, housing stability and economic well-being, and health and safety. None of the outcomes in the education and training and social support domains was statistically significant. One secondary outcome was favorable and statistically significant in the criminal involvement domain.

Study Objective and Approach

Within the context presented above, the goal of this study is to provide a rigorous analysis of the costs and benefits of LifeSet. The research team's approach follows best-practice recommendations for performing benefit-cost analyses (BCAs) offered by a National Academy of Sciences panel (Steurle and Jackson, 2016). We build on the foundation of the MDRC evaluation, to understand both the resources required to implement LifeSet—and therefore program costs—and the outcome domains examined and the specific indicators assessed in the two-year evaluation. The estimated impacts from the evaluation represent either benefits or costs, depending on the sign of the impact coefficient, as well as whether the perspective is that of the public sector (i.e., taxpayers), the participants themselves, or the rest of society. In performing a BCA, the goal is to place a monetary value on as many of the known causal effects of the program as possible to ensure a complete accounting of the value of the outcomes affected by the program. In conducting the BCA for LifeSet, we adopt the societal perspective, thereby accounting for the costs and benefits that accrue to participants, the public sector, and private citizens. The resulting analysis of benefits and costs will inform decisionmakers at Youth Villages and elsewhere regarding the potential for a positive return to society from investing in the LifeSet model.

We view our analysis as a *retrospective* BCA, meaning that we estimate costs and benefits as measured in the context of delivering and evaluating the program in Tennessee in the period from 2010 to 2012.[2] We present results in 2015 dollars, the same year as the MDRC cost analysis for the LifeSet evaluation (Skemer and Valentine, 2016). Our approach differs from a *prospective* BCA of LifeSet, such as the one conducted by the Washington State Institute for Public Policy (WSIPP). The WSIPP analysis assumes implementation of LifeSet in Washington state, based on a BCA model the institute developed to analyze the costs and benefits of

---

[2] By contrast, a *prospective* BCA is performed for a program that has yet to be implemented, as a forecast of the expected costs and benefits if an intervention with specific features were to be implemented in a given community for a specified population. Thus, for a prospective BCA, the cost analysis is not based on having already implemented the program but is based on estimates of the resources that are assumed to be required for program implementation and the total cost of those resources. In a prospective analysis, estimates of the likely impacts from delivering the program are typically based on evaluation evidence from similar interventions implemented and evaluated in other contexts (e.g., during an earlier period, in another community, for a similar population). Often, meta-analysis techniques are used to generate expected impact estimates across multiple evaluations of a given program model. After the program is implemented, a retrospective BCA may be performed to assess the accuracy of the prospective BCA.

programs in an array of policy domains (WSIPP, 2018b). The WSIPP BCA methods and results for LifeSet are summarized in Appendix A and discussed later in the report in comparison with the findings from our retrospective analysis.

Road Map for the Report

The next chapter begins with a summary of the estimated costs and impacts for LifeSet based on the MDRC evaluation. Given the array of outcomes measured, Chapter 3 presents the approach taken in this study to value the outcomes examined in the impact evaluation. The resulting estimates of benefits and costs are presented in Chapter 4. Conclusions and implications of the findings are the subject of the final chapter. Additional documentation is provided in the appendixes.

2. Evidence of Cost and Outcomes for LifeSet

As noted in Chapter 1, MDRC evaluated LifeSet in Tennessee using a randomized control trial (RCT) design (Valentine, Skemer, and Courtney, 2015; Skemer and Valentine, 2016).[3] From October 2010 to October 2012, the study enrolled 1,322 transitional youth, ages 18 to 24, who had been in custody with Tennessee's Department of Children's Services for at least 365 days after age 14 or at least one day after age 17. At the time of the evaluation, the program was known as Youth Villages Transitional Living Program. For simplicity, we continue to refer to the program as LifeSet.

Individuals who met the eligibility requirements were randomly assigned to the treatment group ($N = 788$), which was offered LifeSet, or a control group ($N = 534$), which received a list of social service resources available in their community but not offered by LifeSet. A comparison of the baseline characteristics between the treatment and control groups shows that randomization was successful (Manno et al., 2014), with few statistically significant differences in the observed characteristics of the treatment and control groups. The evaluation was an intent-to-treat design, and the participation rate in any LifeSet services was near universal: 99 percent of the group randomly assigned to receive LifeSet participated in at least one transitional living service, 98 percent completed an initial treatment plan, and 95 percent participated in at least one transitional living session (Valentine, Skemer, and Courtney, 2015). Fewer participants ever received a support payment (38 percent), in which are funds provided to LifeSet participants on an as-needed basis to cover basic needs and living expenses. In the year after random assignment, treatment group members who participated in at least one session spent an average of 34 hours in the sessions and participated in an average of 27 sessions. At the end of one year, 41 percent of the treatment group had successfully completed the program and been discharged. Another 32 percent had been discharged without completing the program or with an unknown completion status, while 27 percent had not yet been discharged.

The accompanying implementation study for LifeSet (Manno et al., 2014) indicated that the program, operating out of 13 offices throughout Tennessee, was implemented as intended across the sites, although the local context varied considerably, including the social services infrastructure available to the participants. This, in turn, affected the nature of the services offered by the LifeSet staff. The frequency and duration of services utilized were close to expected levels, participation rates on the part of young adults were high, and participants were highly engaged in services.

[3] This chapter provides a summary of the MDRC evaluation of LifeSet. Additional details about the LifeSet program as implemented in Tennessee, the methods for the RCT evaluation, and the detailed findings from the implementation and impact studies are found in the evaluation reports (Manno et al., 2014; Valentine, Skemer, and Courtney, 2015; Skemer and Valentine, 2016).

In the remainder of this chapter, we draw on the MDRC evaluation reports to review the estimated cost of delivering LifeSet and the estimated program impacts.

Estimated Total Cost of LifeSet in the MDRC Evaluation

The MDRC evaluation provided an estimate of the LifeSet cost (Skemer and Valentine, 2016) but noted that the cost estimate is *gross* rather than net of the cost of services for the control group. For example, although 75 percent of the group randomly assigned to receive LifeSet received help from a case manager, so did 44 percent of the young adults in the control group. Control group members also received help planning for their future education, obtaining employment, managing finances, obtaining housing, and developing life skills. In each case, the rate of service receipt is lower for the control group members, compared with those in the treatment group, but their receipt of services is not zero. This fact is important later when discussing the BCA: Just as the impact estimates are relative to the outcomes for the control group, the estimated program cost should also be relative to the cost of the "business as usual" services received by the control group.

Otherwise, the cost estimate is inclusive in terms of accounting for the salaries and benefits of the LifeSet program staff (e.g., specialists, the clinical supervisor) and administrative staff, as well as costs for operations and maintenance, travel, corporate overhead, and direct financial support to LifeSet young adults. The estimated total gross cost per participant for LifeSet as implemented in Tennessee was $11,841 in 2015 dollars.

Estimated Impacts of LifeSet in the MDRC Evaluation

The MDRC evaluation measured impacts for LifeSet based on a survey of treatment and control group members one year after each study member's enrollment (covering the period from October 2011 through October 2013, given the two-year enrollment period, and denoted as year 1; Valentine, Skemer, and Courtney, 2015) and based on administrative data that allowed measurement of some outcomes at the end of year 1, at the end of year 2, and over the combined year 1 and year 2 period (Skemer and Valentine, 2016). MDRC classified outcomes in the following six domains: education and training, employment and earnings, housing stability and economic well-being, health and safety, social support, and criminal involvement.

Table 2.1 provides a summary of the findings in the form of a stoplight chart, with each row summarizing the impacts for a given outcome measure at three points in time: year 1, year 2, and the combined two-year period. (Detailed results with the magnitude and statistical significance of the impact estimates are provided in a series of tables in Appendix B.) Cells in which the outcome was not measured (e.g., education attainment in year 2 or the combined year 1–year 2 period) are shaded with dark gray. For cells with an impact estimate, the direction of the impact (i.e., the difference between the treatment and control groups) is denoted as an increase (+) or decrease (–). When the estimate was zero or very small (less than half a percentage point change), the cell is marked with a zero.

Table 2.1. Summary of Estimated Impacts by Domain and Year

Outcome	Year 1	Year 2	Combined Year 1 and Year 2
Education and training			
Has high school diploma or GED	+		
Participated in vocational training	+		
Enrolled in postsecondary education*	0	–	–
Enrolled in 4-year college*	0		–
Enrolled in 2-year college*	+		–
Employment and earnings			
Earnings (self-reported)	+		
Earnings (Unemployment Insurance [UI] records)	+	+	+
Earnings of $2,500 or more (UI records)	+	+	
Earnings of $5,000 or more (UI records)	+	+	
Earnings of $7,500 or more (UI records)	+	+	
Employment rate (self-reported, UI records)*	+	+	+
Housing stability and economic well-being			
Score on housing instability scale	–		
Experienced homelessness*	–		
Couch-surfed*	–		
Was unable to pay rent*	–		
Lost housing because unable to pay rent*	–		
Score on economic hardship scale	–		
Did not have necessary clothing/shoes*	–		
Was unable to pay utility bill*	–		
Gas/electricity shut off because unable to pay*	–		
Phone service shut off because unable to pay*	–		
Delayed paying a bill to buy food*	–		
Savings*	–		
Debt*	–		
Received Supplemental Security Income (SSI)*	+		
Received Supplemental Nutrition Assistance Program (SNAP)*	+		
Received Special Supplemental Nutrition Program for Women, Infants, and Children (WIC)*	+		
Received public housing/rental assistance*	+		
Received Families First (Temporary Assistance for Needy Families [TANF])*	–		
Health and safety			
Mental health problem scale	–		
Self-reported general health*	+		
Had a regular source of care*	+		
Received a physical exam*	+		
Received a dental exam*	+		
Did not receive care when needed*	–		
Had health insurance coverage*	+		

Outcome	Year 1	Year 2	Combined Year 1 and Year 2
Health and safety, continued			
Binge drinking in past month	0		
Used illegal drugs	–		
Condom use during last sexual encounter	+		
Was robbed or assaulted	0		
Partner violence	–		
Social support			
Score on social support scale	+		
Very close to an adult	+		
Frequency of contact with caring adult*	+		
Frequency of in-person contact with caring adult*	+		
Feelings of closeness toward caring adult*	+		
Score on familial closeness scale*	+		
Biological family member would offer place to stay*	+		
Friends would offer place to stay*	+		
Criminal involvement			
Criminal behavior scale	0		
Got in gang fight or assault*	+		
Committed property crime*	–		
Carried a handgun*	+		
Sold or helped sell illegal drugs*	+		
Received cash/goods in exchange for sex*	–		
Spent 1 or more nights in jail/prison	–		
Arrested	–	–	0
Convictions	+	+	+
Convicted of felony*			+
Convicted of misdemeanor*			0
Convicted of violent crime*			+
Convicted of property crime*			+
Convicted of drug crime*			–
Convicted of public-order crime*			–

SOURCES: Valentine, Skemer, and Courtney, 2015; Skemer and Valentine, 2016. See Tables B.1 to B.8 in Appendix B for more details.
NOTES: The direction of impacts for the treatment group compared with the control group is denoted as an increase (+) or decrease (–). Impacts can be viewed as favorable (green shading), unfavorable (red shading), or indeterminate (mixed red and green shading). Effects that are smaller than 0.5 percentage points are shown as 0. Darker shading (relevant for green shading and mixed red and green shading only) indicates that outcomes are statistically significant at the 5 percent level or better. Asterisks denote secondary outcomes. Outcomes that are not measured are shaded in dark gray. GED = general equivalency diploma.

Outcome labels marked with an asterisk denote outcomes considered to be secondary in the evaluation design. In the case of the several scales included in the outcome set (e.g., housing instability scale), the table lists the result for the scale and also the individual survey items that make up the scale, which typically are treated as secondary outcomes.

In some cases, a negative impact is actually a favorable outcome (e.g., a reduction in criminal activity), while a positive impact is unfavorable (e.g., an increase in criminal activity). Thus, we color code the directional effects using green shading (favorable) and red shading (unfavorable). For some outcomes, such as the use of social welfare programs, a positive effect may be viewed as favorable (participants obtained greater access to the government benefits for which they qualified as a result of LifeSet) or unfavorable (participants in LifeSet were more dependent on government benefits), depending on the viewpoint of the decisionmaker. In such cases, the cell is shaded in a red and green pattern and viewed as *indeterminant* when judging whether the impact is advantageous or not.

Finally, Table 2.1 also indicates statistical significance. Darker shading indicates that the impact estimate is statistically significant at the 5 percent level or better.

Table 2.1 indicates that results through year 2 are available for education enrollment measures, employment and earnings measures, and criminal involvement measures in the administrative data. A few impacts in these three domains, plus all of the impacts in the other five domains, are based on the year 1 survey data. Key findings from Table 2.1 include the following:

- **Overall.** The direction of effects for the majority of outcomes is favorable: There are more green-shaded than red-shaded cells. At the same time, relatively few of the impact estimates meet the standard threshold for statistical significance ($p < 0.05$ percent, or the 95 percent confidence level).
- **Education and training**. The effect of LifeSet on educational attainment and enrollment was not statistically significant, although several coefficients are in the favorable direction—attaining a high school diploma or GED, enrollment in a two-year college, and participation in vocational training, all in year 1. By year 2, the postsecondary enrollment effects are not in the desired direction, although they are not statistically significant.
- **Employment and earnings**. The impact on self-reported earnings in the first year was positive and statistically significant, as was the effect on the share with earnings of $25,000 or more in year 1 and year 2. There are no statistically significant impacts on the employment rate.
- **Housing stability**. LifeSet had statistically significant favorable effects on measures of housing stability captured in year 1 only, specifically for rates of homelessness and couch-surfing, two indicators in the housing instability scale that also improved and were statistically significant.
- **Economic well-being**. Among the measures of economic well-being, all available only for year 1, the program had a significant favorable effect on hardship, both as captured in the scale and for two specific items: not having necessary clothing or shoes and delaying paying a bill to buy food. Savings and debt measures showed opposite effects (unfavorable and favorable, respectively), although neither was statistically significant. Among the five types of means-tested cash or in-kind benefits, most showed a positive impact, which could be viewed favorably or unfavorably, as noted earlier. Receipt of SNAP benefits was the only program with a statistically significant effect.
- **Health, safety, and social support**. The health, safety, and social support outcomes were generally in the favorable direction, although statistically significant only for the mental health problems scale, the indicator of not receiving health care when needed, and the indicator of experiencing partner violence.

- **Criminal involvement**. The category of criminal involvement shows mixed findings, again with few statistically significant effects, but several in the unfavorable direction. The only statistically significant effect was a favorable (negative) impact on receiving cash or goods in exchange for sex. The estimates show an unfavorable (positive) impact on convictions across years, although not statistically significant. The impact on arrests, on the other hand, was in the favorable direction, but again not statistically significant.

In sum, as noted in the year 2 follow-up MDRC evaluation report (Skemer and Valentine, 2016, p. 33):

> On average, based on all available data, including both Year 1 survey data and Year 2 administrative data, the program price tag of nearly $12,000 per sample member purchases modest increases in employment and earnings, reductions in homelessness and couch-surfing, reductions in experiences of economic hardship, improvements in mental health, and reductions in experiences of partner violence. These gains may also have resulted in benefits for society as a whole in the form of reductions in the use of homeless shelters and mental health services, among other benefits. However, the cost of the program does not purchase any improvements in the areas of education, criminal involvement, or social support.

In the chapters that follow, we more formally assess the comparison of LifeSet program cost with the value of the program outcomes.

3. Valuing the Outcomes from LifeSet

In this chapter, we document our approach to valuing as many of the outcomes, both primary and secondary, as possible that are measured in the MDRC evaluation of LifeSet, drawing on the impact findings documented in the tables and citations in Appendix B.[4] Our approach is summarized in Table 3.1. Although we are able to value many of the outcomes measured in the MDRC evaluation, there are others for which estimates of economic value are not readily available. The outcomes omitted from valuation are noted in the BCA results presented in the next chapter.

We discuss our approach to valuing outcomes by domain, where housing instability, economic well-being, health, and safety are treated as separate domains.

Education and Training

This first domain captures the effects of participation in LifeSet on education attainment at the secondary level and enrollment at the postsecondary level, based on a combination of data from the 12-month survey and administrative data from the National Student Clearinghouse (NSC) covering two years (see the MDRC evaluation for details). Impacts on participation in vocation training are also observed, based on the 12-month survey. After one year, LifeSet participants had a higher incidence of having a high school diploma and enrollment in vocational training, but the estimates of postsecondary enrollment showed a lower incidence by the end of two years for LifeSet participants relative to the control group (see Table B.1). Thus, measured educational attainment at the secondary level favors the treatment group, while potential attainment at the postsecondary level (actual postsecondary certificates or degrees are not observed) appears to favor the control group. We estimate the potential economic consequences in two stages.

[4] In many cases, the outcomes considered to be primary are scales based on multiple secondary outcomes. For purposes of valuation, we focus on the individual secondary outcomes rather than the scales.

Table 3.1. Sources of Shadow Values for LifeSet Impacts in MDRC Evaluation

Outcome	Impacts in MDRC Evaluation	Source for Shadow Price
Education and training		
Attainment (diploma/GED)	Year 1	Estimate lifetime earnings gain for individuals in Tennessee with a high school degree versus no degree based on the CPS; apply Cohen and Piquero (2009) assumptions for the value of fringe benefits and nonmarket benefits relative to earnings gains (range)
Participated in vocational training	Year 1	Not valued
Enrolled in postsecondary education*	Year 1, Year 2	Estimate lifetime earnings gain for individuals in Tennessee with some college versus a high school degree based on the CPS; apply Cohen and Piquero (2009) assumptions for the value of fringe benefits and nonmarket benefits relative to earnings gains (range); apply estimated cost of postsecondary education
Employment and earnings		
Earnings (self-reported, UI records)	Year 1, Year 2	Observed earnings gains are valued in dollars for years 1 and 2 (range); future earnings gains are based on educational attainment effect (above)
Employment rate (self-reported, UI records)*	Year 1, Year 2	Captured in observed and projected earnings
Housing stability and economic well-being		
Housing instability (homelessness, couch-surfing)	Year 1	Average cost of individual homelessness spell from Spellman et al. (2010) (range)
Economic hardship	Year 1	Nonpecuniary value not captured
Savings*	Year 1	Not valued
Debt*	Year 1	Not valued
Received SSI*	Year 1	Value of monthly federal SSI benefit for one adult recipient; assume 4 and 8 months of use for range; only administrative cost from societal perspective
Received SNAP*	Year 1	Value of monthly federal SNAP benefit for one adult recipient; otherwise same assumptions as SSI
Received WIC*	Year 1	Value of monthly federal WIC benefit for one adult/one child recipient; otherwise same assumptions as SSI
Received public housing/rental assistance*	Year 1	Value of monthly Tennessee housing benefit (voucher) for one adult recipient; otherwise same assumptions as SSI
Received Families First (TANF)*	Year 1	Value of monthly Tennessee TANF benefit for one adult/one child recipient; otherwise same assumptions as SSI

Outcome	Impacts in MDRC Evaluation	Source for Shadow Price
Health and safety		
Mental health problems	Year 1	Not valued
Self-reported general health*	Year 1	Not valued
Had a regular source of care*	Year 1	Not valued
Received a physical exam, dental exam*	Year 1	Not valued
Did not receive care when needed*	Year 1	Not valued
Had health insurance coverage*	Year 1	Not valued
Binge drinking in past month	Year 1	Use estimate from Spoth, Guyll, and Day (2002) on lifetime cost per alcohol-use-disordered individual
Used illegal drugs	Year 1	Not valued
Condom use during last sexual encounter	Year 1	Not valued
Was robbed or assaulted	Year 1	Estimate from Roman (2011) of social cost of crime for assault (includes pain and suffering)
Partner violence	Year 1	Estimate from Roman (2011) of social cost of crime for assault (includes pain and suffering)
Social support		
Social support	Year 1	Not valued
Closeness/contact with caring adult	Year 1	Not valued
Score on familial closeness scale*	Year 1	Not valued
Biological family member would offer place to stay*	Year 1	Not valued
Friends would offer place to stay*	Year 1	Not valued
Criminal involvement		
Criminal behavior scale	Year 1	Captured in valuation of specific crime categories
Got in gang fight or assault*	Year 1	Estimate from Cohen and Piquero (2009) of social cost of crime for simple assault (includes pain and suffering)
Committed property crime*	Year 1	Estimate from Cohen and Piquero (2009) of social cost of crime for property crime/vandalism (includes pain and suffering)
Carried a handgun*	Year 1	Not valued
Sold or helped sell illegal drugs*	Year 1	Estimate from Cohen and Piquero (2009) of social cost of crime for drug crimes (includes pain and suffering)
Received cash/goods in exchange for sex*	Year 1	Estimate from Cohen and Piquero (2009) of social cost of crime for prostitution (includes pain and suffering)
Spent 1 or more nights in jail/prison	Year 1	Included in crime cost
Arrested	Year 1, Year 2	Included in crime cost
Convictions (overall, by type)	Year 1, Year 2	Included in crime cost

SOURCE: Table 2.1.
NOTES: CPS = Current Population Survey. Impacts can be viewed as favorable (green shading), unfavorable (red shading), or indeterminate (mixed red and green shading). Darker shading (relevant for green shading and mixed red and green shading only) indicates that outcomes are statistically significant at the 5 percent level or better. Asterisks denote secondary outcomes.

First, we estimate the effects on lifetime earnings, fringe benefits, and nonmarket educational benefits for the LifeSet participants from their observed higher rate of high school attainment as of the first year. We focus on receipt of a high school diploma and assume no benefit from attaining a GED.[5] To estimate the lifetime earnings gain of a recipient of a high school diploma relative to a dropout, we use annual earnings data for individuals in Tennessee from the pooled 2009 to 2013 CPS (see U.S. Census Bureau, undated). Using the estimated median annual earnings at each age, we estimate the present discounted value of lifetime earnings from ages 21 to 65 by education level. After converting to 2015 dollars using the Consumer Price Index (CPI) and assuming a 3 percent discount rate, we estimate that the present-value lifetime earnings gain for a Tennessee high school graduate compared with a dropout to be $245,749.[6] To measure the effect on total compensation, we assume that fringe benefits add another 25 percent of the value of the earnings differential. We further assume the nonmarket benefits of higher educational attainment, such as improvements in health and reductions in crime and delinquency, to be 50 to 100 percent of the value of the direct earnings gains, thereby producing a more conservative and less conservative estimate of the nonmarket benefits from higher educational attainment. The fringe benefit rate and estimated nonmarket benefits are consistent with parameters used by Cohen and Piquero (2009) in their estimate, respectively, of the market and nonmarket effects of dropping out of high school. The final step is to apply the 3.2 percentage point increase in the high school diploma rate to estimate the total labor market and non–labor market benefits for LifeSet participants from their higher rate of high school degree attainment, observed after one year.

Second, we adopt a similar method to account for the lower enrollment rate of LifeSet participants in postsecondary education. Based on the CPS, we estimate that individuals in Tennessee with some college education have higher lifetime present-value earnings than high school graduates: $159,998 more, in 2015 dollars. We make the same assumptions regarding the value of fringe benefits relative to earnings (25 percent) and the value of nonmarket benefits of higher education relative to the earnings gain (50 to 100 percent). For postsecondary education, we also need to account for the added educational cost, which we assume to be $10,000 over two years.

It is important to note that, for purposes of the BCA, we treat these estimated lifetime labor market and non–labor market benefits as unobserved outcomes, based on education impacts

---

[5] There is debate in the economics literature about the economic returns to obtaining a GED versus a high school diploma. For example, Heckman and LaFontaine (2006) and Heckman, Humphries, and Mader (2011) find no benefit in the labor market of a GED, compared with a regular diploma, after accounting for the selectivity of who receives which type of diploma and other biases introduced by the available data. The CPS, our source of estimated lifetime earnings, does not differentiate between those who completed a high school degree via a regular diploma versus a GED.

[6] This figure accords with other estimates in the literature. For example, Cohen and Piquero (2009) estimate the lifetime present-value earnings differential for high school graduates versus dropouts as of 2007 to be about $280,000, at the national level.

estimated after one or two years following enrollment in LifeSet. If educational attainment equalizes for the treatment and control groups in the future, the estimated lifetime earnings effects are likely overstated, whether to the advantage of LifeSet participants (from higher high school graduation rates) or to nonparticipants (from higher enrollment in postsecondary education). Relative to the estimated economic values of observed outcomes, these projected lifetime benefits should be viewed as more uncertain.

We also note that we did not estimate the lifetime labor market and non–labor market benefits from the higher rate of participation in vocational training on the part of LifeSet participants. Because of methodological challenges, few studies provide causal estimates of the economic value of vocational training, and the available estimates vary considerably (Leuven and Oosterbeek, 2008; Rzepka, 2018). Furthermore, without more information about the nature of the training and whether a certificate or other credential was awarded, there is too much uncertainty to produce a valid estimate.

Employment and Earnings

The LifeSet impact evaluation estimated increased employment incidence and increased earnings for program participants relative to the control group, based on both 12-month survey data and two years of administrative data, although estimates were statistically significant only for earnings. We assume that the primary economic value in this domain derives from the earnings gains and use the two data sources to capture earnings gains for either the first year only (based on the 12-month survey) or for the first two years (based on the administrative records). The survey data produced an estimated observed earnings gain of $611 in the first year, while the administrative data showed a gain of $224 for the first year and $103 for the second year (see Table B.2). After converting the earnings gains to 2015 dollars and discounting the second-year gains (administrative data only) by one year, the estimated range of the earnings impacts is from $225 (the more conservative estimate, based on the earnings records) to $631 (the less conservative estimate, based on the survey data).

To avoid double counting, we did not use these estimated impacts on earnings to project future earnings gains. Rather, the projected earnings gains are based on the impacts for educational attainment, discussed earlier.

Housing Stability

The MDRC evaluation reported the impact of LifeSet, in the first year, on a housing stability scale composed of four indicators: experiencing homelessness, experiencing couch-surfing, being unable to pay rent, and losing housing because of the inability to pay rent. The indicators are all measuring whether the type of instability was experienced during the past year but not the frequency (such as the number of nights spent homeless or spent couch-surfing). For each indicator and for the scale overall, LifeSet participants had better outcomes (statistically significant for two of the four indicators and the overall scale), which would presumably generate nonmonetary benefits for the young adults, as well as spillover benefits for the public sector in the form of reduced reliance on shelters and also private benefits for the friends or family who do not need to provide temporary housing.

As with other potential nonpecuniary (or psychic) benefits, we did not identify valid dollar estimates to apply to the indicators of reduced housing instability.[7] We did estimate the dollar benefits from reduced use of homeless shelters, assuming that shelter use was brief. In particular, Spellman et al. (2010) estimate the cost to the homeless system for individuals who use emergency shelters for one or two brief stays, totaling one to three weeks, as $321 to $686 in 2006 dollars. We use the CPI to convert those estimates to 2015 dollars. Given the estimated impact of a 6.1 percentage point reduction in experiencing homelessness (see Table B.3), this produces an estimated range of benefits from $23 (the more conservative estimate) to $49 (the less conservative estimate). We did not assume that the effects on housing instability persisted beyond the first-year impacts.

Economic Well-Being

The indicators of economic well-being show both favorable and unfavorable effects, with a significant reduction in the scale of economic hardship and mixed but largely small and statistically insignificant effects on savings, debt, and use of cash and in-kind means-tested transfers. The economic hardship indicators and overall scale are not readily translated into dollar values, whether the direct nonpecuniary aspects of hardship (e.g., the psychic cost of not having necessary clothing or shoes or not being able to pay for utilities or phone service) or the indirect consequences of these types of hardship for other life course outcomes, such as employment, education enrollment, or risky behaviors. The indirect consequences will be captured to the extent that they are manifested in other key outcomes measured in the evaluation, such as employment and earnings and education enrollment.

In the case of receipt of public benefits, we account for the dollar value of the transfer benefit as it would apply for a single adult (or family with one adult and one dependent child, in the case of WIC and TANF) in Tennessee as of 2015 (see Table 3.2). Because the evaluation measured any use of the benefit program during the first year after randomization but not the months of use, we assume that benefits were used for a minimum of four months and a maximum of eight months to get a range of dollar values (from more conservative to less conservative, respectively). From the societal perspective, the value of the transfer has a zero-sum effect between the participant and the public sector, except for the administrative costs (a savings when benefit use declines or an added cost when benefit use increases). For the less conservative

[7] By *nonpecuniary* or *psychic costs* (or benefits), we are referring to outcomes that are not expressed in monetary terms, such as stress, emotional distress, pain and suffering, and other adverse aspects of well-being (or quality of life) on the cost side or happiness, contentment, security, and other positive aspects of well-being on the benefit side.

assumption, we make a standard assumption that administrative costs are 10 percent of the benefit amount (Karoly, 2008). As a more conservative assumption, we assume a 20 percent administrative cost rate. Because the impacts on the incidence of benefit receipt were generally small (see Table B.4) and only administrative costs are recognized from the societal perspective, the estimated dollar savings or cost in the BCA are generally small and offsetting (use increases for some benefit programs but decreases for others). We do not project potential future effects on benefit use beyond the one-year effects estimated in the evaluation.

Again, to the extent that participation in transfer programs has other intended or unintended consequences on employment, earnings, and other aspects of well-being, those indirect effects will be captured in our direct estimates of the effects of LifeSet on those outcomes and valued accordingly.

Table 3.2. Parameter Assumptions for Public Benefit Programs

Type of Public Benefit	Assumed Range of Months of Use	Monthly Benefit Amount[a]	Assumed Administrative Cost Rate	Source for Benefit Amount
SSI		$733	10% and 20%	Social Security Administration (undated)
SNAP	Minimum = 4 Maximum = 8	$194	10% and 20%	U.S. Department of Agriculture (2015)
WIC		$43	10% and 20%	Bitler and Karoly (2015)
Public housing/rental assistance		$435	10% and 20%	Carlson et al. (2011)
Families First (TANF)		$142	10% and 20%	Urban Institute (undated)

[a] Benefit amount is for the federal or Tennessee-specific benefit, as of 2015. The assistance unit is assumed to be a single adult, except for WIC and TANF, where we assume a single adult with one dependent child. The benefit amount is the maximum before any benefit reductions, except for housing, which is an estimated average value of the housing benefit that varies by local rental rates and family income.

Health

The MDRC evaluation assessed various measures of health status, health care utilization, and health insurance coverage, with estimates of positive impacts on all measures, although effects were statistically significant only in the case of the mental health scale and not receiving care when needed (see Table B.5). Given the nature of the outcomes measured, none could be readily valued in dollar terms. The scale of mental health problems was not a diagnostic measure of one or more mental health disorders, so it could not be linked to the expected savings in health care use or the nonpecuniary benefits from improvements in a mental health condition. The improvement in self-reported health is likewise not sufficiently specific to value. Having a regular source of care and having health insurance would imply an increased use of health care services (some of which may be covered by the public sector), consistent with the higher incidence of having a physical exam and a dental exam. These increased costs could be potentially valued, but the dollar amounts would be small, given the size of the increased incidence (a few percentage points). Any resulting improvements in health from the greater access to and use of care would ideally be valued as well, but there is insufficient information on how health status improved, as already noted.

All of the health indicators may have spillover consequences for outcomes that were measured in the evaluation and captured in the BCA, such as the effects on participation in education, labor market outcomes, and use of social welfare programs. Thus, these indirect effects in this domain will be captured in the BCA.

Safety

The safety domain captures substance use, risky sexual behavior, and crime victimization. The estimated impacts for LifeSet participants for these outcomes were generally small or zero and statistically significant only in the case of partner violence (also known as *intimate partner violence*). We valued the measure of alcohol use disorder based on the estimate in Spoth, Guyll, and Day (2002) of the present-value lifetime cost per alcohol-use-disordered individual, a value of $119,633 in 1992 dollars or $202,103 in 2015 dollars. Because of the small effect size associated with the impact on binge drinking in the past month and further attenuation of the effect size to correspond with an effect on lifetime disordered alcohol use, the estimated dollar benefit is a range of just $44 to $89.

We did not directly value the effect on the use of illegal drugs but consider that impact to be indirectly captured in the estimated nonmarket benefits of educational attainment (discussed earlier). The same is true for reduced sexual risk taking through condom use.

We did estimate the crime costs associated with the effect on being robbed or assaulted (victimization increased by a very small amount) and the effect on intimate partner violence (victimization decreased by a statistically significant amount) (see Table B.6). In both cases, we used the estimate from Roman (2011) of the social cost of crime associated with assault: a range of $66,644 to $134,770 in 2008 dollars, based on a median versus mean estimate (or $73,365 to $148,362 in 2015 dollars). This estimate includes a component for pain and suffering, although the share of the cost for the nonpecuniary victim costs is not separately reported by Roman (2011). In the case of partner violence, given the 6.4 percentage point decrease in the incidence of being in a violent relationship and assuming just one assault, on average, in the 12-month reporting period, the estimated reduction in cost for this crime as a result of participating in LifeSet ranges from $4,695 to $9,495.

Social Support

The measures of social support—which generally showed favorable (although statistically insignificant) impacts in the MDRC evaluation (see Table B.7)—are not valued in the BCA. The assessed indicators of social support from family and friends have the potential to improve well-being both directly (for example, from the psychic value of greater closeness and feeling of being supported) and indirectly (for example, from the manifestations of the support provided, such as access to a place to stay or other forms of material or financial support received). The expectation is that these forms of support would produce private benefits for LifeSet participants. There may also be spillover benefits for the family and friends providing direct support and to the public sector if the privately provided support displaces reliance on public-sector services.

However, there are no readily available estimates of the psychic value for the recipients of social support from family and friends or for the providers of the support. Some of the potential indirect consequences of the improved social support, however, are captured elsewhere in outcomes measured in other domains. For example, the measured reduction in housing instability and the improvement in mental health status may result, in part, from the increase in social support estimated for LifeSet participants. To the extent that we value these indirect effects, they are captured in the BCA. However, the psychic benefits will not be reflected in the estimates.

Criminal Involvement

The LifeSet evaluation captured self-reported criminal activity as part of the 12-month survey, both as a summary scale and indicators of specific types of criminal behavior and as the incidence of arrests and convictions. In addition, administrative data were used to measure arrests and convictions up to two years after randomization. The findings showed mixed impacts on self-reported crime, with only one statistically significant reduction in the incidence of criminal behavior—for receiving cash or goods in exchange for sex (see Table B.8). Although the incidence of arrests was lower (but statistically insignificant) for the LifeSet participants, the incidence of convictions was higher. One drawback of the measures of the incidence of arrests and convictions is that they reflect only the criminal activity that is detected by law enforcement, whereas the self-reported measures potentially include all criminal activity (although self-reports may be subject to underreporting). We focus on valuing the effects of LifeSet on crimes committed based on the self-reports and include the victim cost of crime, as well as the cost to law enforcement and the judicial system and the costs of incarceration associated with each category of crime.

In particular, we rely on estimates from Cohen and Piquero (2009) of the cost of various categories of crime that include criminal justice system costs (accounting for the probability of arrests, convictions, and incarceration), as well as victim costs, such as the cost of injury, lost work time, and the intangible victim costs associated with avoidance behavior and pain and suffering. Lower-bound and upper-bound estimates of costs are available based on alternative estimation methods. Because the evaluation reports the incidence of criminal behavior and not the number of crimes in any given category, our valuation is based on assuming one crime event for the 12-month reporting period. To the extent that the reported incidence is associated with more than one event (for either an estimated decrease or increase in crime), our estimates will be an undervaluation of the total cost of the crime impacts (either savings from reduced crime or added cost from increased crime, respectively).

To avoid double counting, we do not separately value the estimated effects of LifeSet on arrests and convictions that apply only for those crimes detected. The probabilities of detection and associated law enforcement and justice system costs are already included in the Cohen and Piquero (2009) estimates. This may understate some of the system-level costs, to the extent that young adults in the evaluation engaged in criminal behavior outside the types of crime covered in the self-reports, behavior that led to arrests and convictions. However, given the mixed effects of LifeSet on criminal activity, these omitted system-level costs may offset one another if some types of unmeasured crime increased for LifeSet participants while others declined. Furthermore, given the statistically insignificant effects of LifeSet on most types of crime measured in the evaluation, as well as the measures of arrests and convictions, the omitted valuations are likely to be small in magnitude.

4. Comprehensive Benefit-Cost Analysis for LifeSet

In this chapter, we present the results of our BCA, drawing on the cost and impact estimates summarized in Chapter 2 and employing the approach to valuing outcomes reviewed in Chapter 3. Given the uncertainties in both cost and the value of outcomes, our approach produces, in most cases, a more conservative estimate of costs or benefits and a less conservative estimate. This serves to demonstrate the potential range of net benefits associated with LifeSet. We also present a base-case estimate developed from the midpoint between the two bounds.

As noted in Chapter 1, we consider our BCA to be retrospective. Thus, the intervention is LifeSet as implemented and evaluated in Tennessee in 2010 to 2012. Our BCA is performed from the societal perspective, and we use a 3 percent discount rate. Monetary amounts are in 2015 dollars. Table 4.1 presents the results of the BCA discussed in this chapter.

Cost of LifeSet

The MDRC evaluation estimated that total (gross) costs of LifeSet were $11,841 in 2015 dollars (Skemer and Valentine, 2016). As discussed in Appendix C, based on the 12-month survey data collected as part of the evaluation, we estimate that the cost of services received by the control group (i.e., the business-as-usual supports), required resources that would be valued between $3,078 and $3,890 (with a midpoint of about $3,500). Since these estimated costs of the services used by the control group represent an offset to the cost of the services received by the treatment group, the more conservative figure for that offset is the smaller of the two numbers, whereas the less conservative estimate is the larger number (i.e., the less conservative estimate implies a greater offset and therefore a lower net cost for program participation).

As shown in Table 4.1 (top shaded row), this means that the net cost of LifeSet is estimated to range from a high of about $8,800 per participant to as little as just under $8,000 per participant. The base case estimate is about $8,400 per participant.

Benefits (and Costs) from the Estimated Impacts of LifeSet

Table 4.1 shows the estimated present-value benefits associated with the outcomes that we valued, under more and less conservative assumptions, as well as the midpoint (or base-case) estimate. These benefits are divided into two groups (starting at the second and third shaded rows of Table 4.1): those based on observed outcomes and those projected from observed outcomes, with the latter being less certain. For each source of benefits, we indicate whether the impact estimate is based on outcomes measured as of year 1 (i.e., one year after randomization, based on self-reported survey data) or as of year 1 and year 2 (either the sum, in the case of earnings records, or the average over years 1 and 2, in the case of higher education enrollment).

Table 4.1. Estimated Cost and Benefits of LifeSet per Participant Under Alternative Assumptions, 2015 Dollars

Summary Result	More Conservative Estimate	Base-Case Estimate	Less Conservative Estimate
Present-value cost	**8,763**	**8,357**	**7,951**
LifeSet cost	11,841	11,841	11,841
Offset for service utilization by control group	–3,078	–3,484	–3,890
Present-value benefits from observed outcomes	**4,101**	**6,506**	**8,912**
Earnings (observed years 1 and 2; self-report year 1)	225	428	631
Homelessness (year 1)	23	36	49
Social welfare program use (year 1)			
SSI	–23	–15	–6
SNAP	–19	–12	–5
WIC	–1	0	0
Public housing	–11	–7	–3
TANF	2	1	0
Problem alcohol use (year 1)	44	67	89
Victimization (year 1)			
Robbed or assaulted	–147	–222	–297
Partner violence	4,695	7,095	9,495
Criminal behavior (year 1)			
Gang fight or assault	–282	–361	–439
Property crime	18	17	17
Sold or helped sell illegal drugs	–513	–637	–761
Received cash/goods in exchange for sex	88	114	140
Present-value benefits from projected outcomes	**3,976**	**4,885**	**5,794**
High school graduate productivity gain (year 1)	7,864	7,864	7,864
High school graduate fringe benefits (year 1)	1,966	1,966	1,966
High school graduate other nonmarket benefits (year 1)	1,966	4,915	7,864
Postsecondary education cost (years 1–2)	340	340	340
Postsecondary education productivity gain (years 1–2)	–5,440	–5,440	–5,440
Postsecondary education fringe benefits (years 1–2)	–1,360	–1,360	–1,360
Postsecondary education other nonmarket benefits (years 1–2)	–1,360	–3,400	–5,440
Deadweight cost	**–4,368**	**–2,053**	**0**
Present-value net benefits	**–5,055**	**981**	**6,755**
Outcomes not valued			
Vocational education cost, productivity gain, and other benefits	?	?	?
Nonpecuniary cost of housing insecurity	+	+	+
Nonpecuniary cost of economic insecurity	+	+	+
Mental health problems	+	+	+
Health status, insurance coverage, and care utilization	?	?	?
Use of illegal drugs	+	+	+
Use of condoms	+	+	+
Nonpecuniary value of social support	+	+	+
Cost of carrying a handgun	+	+	+

NOTES: A plus sign indicates expected positive present-value net benefits, based on estimated impact. A question mark indicates positive *or* negative expected present-value net benefits, given possible countervailing effects.

Given the mixture of both favorable and unfavorable impacts estimated for LifeSet, the rows for the various outcomes are sometimes negative, indicating greater costs as a result of the program, relative to the counterfactual. This occurs for several of the social welfare programs, in which the estimated program use, based on the survey data, was higher for the LifeSet group. Negative benefits are also estimated for two of the observed crime indicators, because those in the treatment group had a higher incidence relative to the control group. Among the projected outcomes, the higher rate of high school graduation for the LifeSet group produces long-term earnings, fringe benefits, and nonmarket benefits. However, because the control group had higher rates of enrollment in postsecondary education, the projected future benefits from this source of impact are negative and almost offset the high school productivity gains.

Among the observed outcomes, the largest contributor to positive net benefits is the estimated benefit from reducing intimate partner violence. This reflects the favorable and significant effect of the impact of LifeSet on this outcome, as well as the costs of this violence in terms of both pecuniary costs (e.g., medical costs, lost work time) and the harder-to-quantify pain and suffering. The observed earnings effects are also positive but considerably smaller under both more and less conservative assumptions.

Estimated Net Benefits of LifeSet

The bottom-line result, shown in Table 4.1 (final shaded row), is the present-value net benefits derived from subtracting present-value costs from present-value benefits. Under the more conservative assumptions for both costs and the valuation of outcomes (i.e., using the higher cost estimate and the lower benefit estimates), the estimated net benefits are negative: about $5,100 per participant. This means the program expenditures exceeded the benefits that could be valued by this amount. Note that, under these more conservative assumptions, present-value benefits are positive for both observed outcomes and those that are projected into the future. However, part of these positive present-value benefits were offset by the (negative) deadweight cost associated with raising government revenues to pay for the program (second-to-the-last shaded row in Table 4.1). In other words, the program cost and (negative) deadweight loss are not sufficiently offset by the estimated positive benefits.

Under the less conservative assumptions—with the lower estimate of costs, the higher estimate of benefits, and assumed zero deadweight loss—LifeSet is estimated to produce positive net benefits of about $6,800 per participant. This results from a more than doubling of the benefits from observed outcomes (largely through the higher estimate of cost of intimate partner violence and the associated benefits when such violence is reduced). Present-value benefits from projected outcomes are also higher. The value of the observed outcomes, almost $8,900 per participant, would alone be enough to offset the cost of the program, but again these benefits arise from one source: the reduction in intimate partner violence. With this estimate of benefits, the benefit-cost ratio would be 1.85, indicating one dollar and 85 cents in benefits for every dollar of upfront costs.

Using the midpoint of the range of estimated costs and benefits, the LifeSet program is estimated to generate present-value net benefits of almost $1,000 per participant, or a favorable benefit-cost ratio of 1.10. Under the more conservative assumptions, the ratio of benefits to cost is less than 1 (0.42), indicating that costs exceed benefits.

Accounting for Uncertainty in the Included Impacts

The base-case estimates rest on assumptions about the economic values of the outcomes affected by LifeSet, as well as the value of the resources used by the control group. In most cases, there was a range of possible values based on estimates available from the MDRC evaluation or from the research literature. Given this uncertainty, Table 4.1 shows results under more and less conservative assumptions, along with the base case.

There are other sources of uncertainty, such as those associated with the estimated impacts from participating in LifeSet, based on the RCT evaluation. As a further sensitivity analysis, we conducted a Monte Carlo simulation to estimate the likelihood of a positive present-value net benefits estimate based on assumptions about the distribution of both the impact estimates (those reported in Appendix B) and the economic values (those summarized in Table 3.1). That analysis (see Appendix D for details), showed that, in 53 percent of the simulations, net benefits were greater than zero, indicating a positive economic return. This result is consistent with the base-case estimate of a positive per-participant present-value net benefit of about $1,000.

About 25 percent of the simulations fell below the more conservative estimate of net benefits (i.e., more negative than –$5,100 per participant). For about 25 percent of the simulations, the estimated present-value net benefits were even higher than the less conservative estimate (i.e., more positive than $6,800 per participant). This wide range of potential values for the economic return of LifeSet reflects the fact that many of the impact estimates from the MDRC evaluation were not very precisely estimated (and therefore not statistically significant; see Appendix B) and that there was also a wide range in the assumed economic values for some of the outcomes (e.g., the cost of being a victim of a specific crime).

Potential Unmeasured Benefits (and Costs) of LifeSet

As discussed in Chapter 3, we did not find credible estimates to value a number of the outcomes measured in the MDRC evaluation. Thus, the exclusion of other potential unmeasured benefits (and costs) is another source of uncertainty in estimating the economic returns to LifeSet. To call attention to these other possible sources of economic benefits, the bottom panel of Table 4.1 records the set of outcomes that are not valued in the BCA result. In each case, we indicate whether the outcome would be expected to produce benefits (a positive sign), costs (a negative sign), or an unknown valuation (a question mark).

It is evident from the list of omitted outcomes that, with two exceptions, all would produce positive net benefits if they could be valued. These include the nonpecuniary benefits from reduced housing insecurity, reduced economic insecurity, and greater social support; improvements in mental health and reduced substance misuse; reduced costs associated with having a handgun; and greater adherence to safer sex practices. If these outcomes could be valued, they would add to the estimated benefits and could possibly lead to positive net benefits under the more conservative assumptions and would produce an even higher benefit-cost ratio under the base case and the less conservative assumptions.

The two exceptions are the potential benefits from the higher rate of enrollment in vocational education after one year and the combined effect on health status, health insurance coverage, and health care utilization. In the case of the former, the higher rate of enrollment in vocational training on the part of the LifeSet group would need to account for both the cost of the training program and the possibility of some labor market return from the additional training. As noted in Chapter 3, there is uncertainty in the expected returns from vocational training (given that the nature of the training program is not known) and, thus, whether the future labor market returns are sufficient to offset the training cost. More generally, the research literature shows widely varying estimates of the returns to vocational education, depending on the methods used to estimate the earnings effects (Leuven and Oosterbeek, 2008; Rzepka, 2018). Furthermore, there is an expectation that the returns are likely to be highly dependent on the nature of the training program, such as its duration, its quality, and the occupational skills targeted.

In the case of the health-related outcomes, the effect on estimated net benefits is also uncertain, given the pattern of findings from the evaluation. In particular, LifeSet participants were estimated to have better self-reported health, higher rates of health insurance coverage, and greater access to a regular source of care and to have received specific types of care at higher rates (i.e., physician exam and dental exam). Relative to the control group, the health insurance coverage and use of care would be expected to increase costs to the public sector, especially if the health insurance or care provision was publicly subsidized (e.g., through Medicaid). The care received would potentially produce better health outcomes in the short term and potentially in the longer term as well, which could result in cost savings to the public sector in the future. LifeSet participants might also experience private gains from better health in the form of higher earnings, as well as any nonpecuniary benefits from better health outcomes. Whether these gains from improved health outweigh the insurance and care costs is uncertain without more information on the nature of the health care services received, the improvements in health status, and whether the short-term impacts were sustained.

Even with these sources of uncertain net benefits or costs, under the more conservative assumptions, the addition of the currently unmeasured benefits could be sufficient to generate positive net benefits overall. Furthermore, the sources of unmeasured benefits would add to the estimated benefits under the base case and the less conservative assumptions. However, many of the impacts on these outcomes that were not valued were small, which would dampen the magnitude of the unmeasured benefits (or costs). Nevertheless, it is important to keep in mind that the BCA is not able to account for the economic value of all of the outcomes measured in the LifeSet evaluation and may underestimate the overall economic returns.

Comparison of Retrospective BCA with WSIPP Prospective BCA

As noted earlier, LifeSet has also been subject to an economic evaluation as part of a BCA tool developed by WSIPP (WSIPP, 2018b). (See Appendix A for a summary of the WSIPP methods and findings.) The analysis shows costs of just under $10,000 per participant in 2017 dollars and negative net benefits of about $3,100 per participant, for a total present-value net benefits of –$13,000. As discussed in Appendix A, the WSIPP analysis produces a different finding for several key reasons:

- First, the WSIPP analysis is prospective for Washington state and based on a limited set of the outcomes affected by LifeSet, then uses only the first-year impact estimates from the MDRC evaluation (Valentine, Skemer, and Courtney, 2015).
- Second, the estimate of the cost of LifeSet for the BCA by WSIPP does not account for the services used by the control group. This has the effect of raising the marginal cost of LifeSet and thereby decreasing the estimated net benefits, all else equal.
- Third, the WSIPP model is not designed to value all possible outcomes for a program, but rather it values a standardized set of outcomes for an array of programs across multiple human services sectors. The WSIPP model does not value several of the LifeSet outcomes that are a source of positive benefits in Table 4.1, such as the benefits from a reduction in intimate partner violence.

5. Conclusions and Implications

The aim of this study was to conduct a retrospective analysis of the costs and benefits of the LifeSet program, as implemented and evaluated in Tennessee for a cohort of participants who enrolled in the program between October 2010 and October 2012. We relied on estimates of program cost generated by MDRC as part of the RCT evaluation, with an adjustment to account for the use of services by young adults in the control group. Likewise, we used the estimates of program impact published by MDRC (Valentine, Skemer, and Courtney, 2015; Skemer and Valentine, 2016) and attached economic values to outcomes, where feasible. In some cases, the economic impacts were projected to the future, beyond the point of last follow-up. Because the impact estimates were not always favorable for the treatment group, the impacts of LifeSet were associated with both positive benefits and negative benefits (or costs). Given uncertainty in the dollar valuation of the outcomes measured in the evaluation, we produced a more conservative estimate of the total value of the outcomes and a less conservative estimate. The midpoint between the more and less conservative valuations provides a base-case estimate. In this final chapter, we highlight key findings and discuss the implications of the analysis for understanding the economic returns from LifeSet.

Key Findings

The BCA of LifeSet presented in this report produced the following key findings (all monetary values are in present-value 2015 dollars):

- The gross cost of LifeSet per participant, as implemented in Tennessee, was estimated to be about $11,800. After we accounted for upper- and lower-bound estimates of the value of services used by young adults in the control group, we estimated that LifeSet cost $8,000 to $8,800 per participant more than business as usual, or about $8,400, according to the base-case (midpoint) estimate. This is the range of cost estimates that should be compared with the value of the impacts generated by the program when determining the economic return.
- Based on outcome measures for treatment and control group members using a survey at 12 months after randomization and on administrative data capturing outcomes up to two years after randomization, the LifeSet RCT estimated impacts across a range of outcomes in the six domains of focus: education and training, employment and earnings, housing stability and economic well-being, health and safety, social support, and criminal involvement. Many, but not all, of the outcomes could be expressed as dollar benefits or costs.
- For the observed outcomes that could be valued, the estimated present-value net benefits ranged from about $4,100 to $8,900 per participant. The magnitude of these benefits primarily derives from the estimated reduction in victimization cost associated with the statistically significant impact of LifeSet in reducing intimate partner violence. All other

domains of observed impact are associated with small positive or negative benefits (largely because the impact estimates were small and statistically insignificant) that effectively cancel each other out.

- Because of the estimated impacts of LifeSet on educational attainment, future benefits in the form of productivity gains (i.e., higher labor market earnings and fringe benefits), as well as nonmarket benefits (e.g., reductions in crime), were also estimated. These projected outcomes produced positive net benefits, ranging from about $4,000 to $5,800 per participant.
- We also accounted for the deadweight cost associated with the increase in taxes required to pay for LifeSet, net of any increase or decrease in taxes based on the program impacts. A more conservative estimate produces a deadweight cost of about $4,400 per participant, while a less conservative estimate has no such deadweight cost (which would arise if the program were paid for by private funds). The midpoint estimate of deadweight cost falls in between, at $2,100.
- The bottom line, accounting for program cost, net benefits from observed and projected outcomes, and deadweight cost, results in estimated present-value net benefits per participant ranging from –$5,100 to $6,800, with a base-case estimate of about $1,000 per participant. Under the more conservative assumptions, the value of observed and projected benefits is almost sufficient to cover the cost of the program. The assumed deadweight cost accounts for almost all of the estimated negative net benefits. The estimated positive net benefits under the less conservative assumptions result from assuming higher economic values for the affected outcomes and from assuming no deadweight cost.
- Using the less conservative estimate of present-value net benefits results in an estimated benefit-cost ratio of about 1.85, or nearly $2 in benefits for every dollar of cost. This can be viewed as a likely upper bound of the economic returns from LifeSet as implemented and evaluated in Tennessee. The midpoint estimate indicates a favorable benefit-cost ratio of 1.10. Under more conservative assumptions, the ratio is 0.42, indicating that costs exceed benefits.
- In addition to estimating lower-bound (more conservative) and upper-bound (less conservative) estimates of the net benefits, we also performed a Monte Carlo simulation analysis that accounted for uncertainty in both impact estimates and the economic values of the outcomes that could be included in the analysis. In just over one-half of the simulations (53 percent), present-value net benefits exceeded zero, indicating a positive economic return.
- As is often the case with social programs, we could not generate an economic value of all of the outcomes examined in the LifeSet RCT. Outcomes that were not valued include the pecuniary and nonpecuniary values associated with housing insecurity, economic insecurity, mental health, and social support, among others. For most of the omitted outcomes, the direction of the estimated impacts of LifeSet would be expected to produce additional net benefits to society. In the case of the impacts on vocational education and health-related outcomes, the net benefits could be positive, negative, or zero, because there would be increases in both costs and benefits. The overall contribution of these omitted outcomes is therefore uncertain, although likely to be positive if vocational education and investments in health produce positive net benefits in the long run. Nevertheless, because the magnitude of the impacts on the outcomes that are not valued

was typically small and statistically insignificant, these omitted sources of potential benefits are not likely to generate net benefits that are substantially larger than those already included in the estimation.

Implications

As a retrospective analysis, the BCA of LifeSet provides a guide to the likely costs and benefits of implementing the program under current conditions in Tennessee and in other jurisdictions in the United States. At the same time, it is important to keep in mind the factors that may affect both the cost and the benefit sides of the BCA equation for LifeSet implementation in other settings.

Factors Affecting the Cost of LifeSet

If we assume the same combination of resources, the per-participant cost of LifeSet—valued here in 2015 dollars—will be higher in current dollars because of inflation. Viewed prospectively, the per-participant cost would be expected to differ as well because of variation in the use of personnel and other resources for program implementation and because of variation in the cost of those resources across different parts of the country. In any given implementation, costs may be lower to the extent that the program can be implemented more efficiently than it was in Tennessee during the 2010s, where overhead expenses might have been higher because of the infrastructure Youth Villages had in place in its home state.

Youth Villages has replicated the LifeSet model in other communities, and experience indicates that several specific factors affect program costs (Youth Villages, undated). Examples include the following:

- **Staff compensation.** The local cost per day is highly dependent on staffing costs for LifeSet specialists, supervisors, and program directors. Staffing expenses account for 70 to 75 percent of the total cost for the program and are determined by local providers and public agencies, based on existing salary ranges, benefit packages, and the cost of living in local labor markets.
- **Facilities and technology.** Costs associated with office expansion or securing new office or meeting space and the cost of purchasing technology to support field-based staff can vary widely, depending on the availability of existing office space and technology resources in a provider organization or public agency.
- **Travel.** Historically, LifeSet staff have been reimbursed for the mileage associated with job-related travel using their personal vehicles. As LifeSet is expanding into dense urban areas, travel reimbursements may differ as staff utilize public transportation, taxi services, or daily rentals. Some providers issue cars to staff for business travel as opposed to reimbursing for travel in personal vehicles.
- **Wraparound services.** Some jurisdictions have more resources available to support young people with immediate needs. In markets where LifeSet is funded partially through private funders, more funding may be specifically dedicated toward tangible goods and

financial support around housing, clothing, and basic necessities. In other areas, staff may have access to limited wraparound funds to aid young people with emergency needs.

- **Organizational infrastructure and supports.** The availability of organizational supports and executive leadership dedicated to supporting LifeSet implementation varies across implementing providers. Some organizations have a robust infrastructure supporting the LifeSet team (e.g., finance, marketing, research and evaluation, program improvement), while others do not. This variation in indirect costs affects the total cost of LifeSet.
- **Program scale.** LifeSet programs that operate with multiple teams can create efficiencies in staff ratios (specifically around director-level support), case assignments, and caseloads. Organizations that are newly implementing LifeSet will often find a higher cost per day during the initial implementation year while ramping up staff and caseloads.

Factors Affecting the Outcomes and Economic Returns of LifeSet

Provided that the resulting impacts from implementing LifeSet would be at least as large as those estimated for Tennessee, if not larger, with a more streamlined personnel structure and more efficient use of other resources, the expected economic returns could be even higher than those estimated for the program's implementation in Tennessee. On the one hand, in higher-cost states or local jurisdictions, the cost per participant of implementing LifeSet could be higher, even after accounting for inflation, because personnel and other resources are more expensive. On the other hand, in such jurisdictions, the economic value of the resulting outcomes may also be higher, such that economic returns could still be positive (assuming that the less conservative assumptions about the value of the impacts of LifeSet hold).

The estimated returns in other settings would also differ to the extent that the impacts of LifeSet diverge from those estimated in the Tennessee RCT. Variation in program impacts may result from improvements in the program model, from differences in the population served and the outcomes those young adults experience under the status quo, and from the existing services available to the LifeSet target population in a given community. In particular, Youth Villages has continued to refine the LifeSet model from the version that was implemented and evaluated in Tennessee, drawing on the latest evidence-based practices for serving the targeted young adults to ensure the strongest possible benefits. Thus, the program's effectiveness might have improved over time. In addition, young adults who experienced more-adverse events prior to enrolling in LifeSet, compared with those served in the Tennessee LifeSet program, could experience even better outcomes from participating in LifeSet than those realized for the Tennessee participants. This would occur if the program model were effective at serving youth with even greater challenges. (Program effects could be smaller for a more at-risk program if the program is not designed to meet the greater challenges of a more vulnerable group.[8]) Likewise, young adults in

[8] Targeted programs may be more or less effective in serving a more disadvantaged group relative to a more advantaged group. On the one hand, there is more room to make a difference in the lives of the most vulnerable youth. On the other hand, the program might not be sufficiently intensive or comprehensive to effectively serve

a community with fewer existing services may also experience greater gains. Conversely, if the population served is less vulnerable in terms of prior adverse experiences or the existing services already provide similar supports, there may be less room for LifeSet to improve outcomes relative to the business-as-usual conditions.

Ultimately, the retrospective BCA of LifeSet presented in this study tells us what costs and benefits were in the Tennessee context and gives us some expectation of what we might see in other settings, but the estimated economic return for Tennessee is not a guarantee of what would be realized in other settings. Any prospective analysis of the costs and benefits of implementing LifeSet under current conditions in a given jurisdiction would need to carefully consider the likely cost of implementing the model with fidelity in that setting, the characteristics and current outcomes of the population to be served, and the availability and effectiveness of existing services available to the target young adults in the community of interest.

Strengthening the Evidence of Economic Returns

As Youth Villages seeks to improve implementation of LifeSet and disseminate the model to other communities, future RCTs could demonstrate the generalizability of the findings from the Tennessee evaluation with respect to program cost, impacts, and net economic benefits. This analysis suggests several steps that Youth Villages could take in future evaluations to strengthen the evidence regarding the program's economic benefits, in particular. These steps include the following:

- Collect comprehensive information on the cost of program implementation, ideally using the ingredients method (Levin and McEwan, 2001), for both the services provided to LifeSet participants and the business-as-usual services taken up by the control group. This insight into the cost of implementation would support the accurate estimation of the incremental cost of LifeSet relative to the status quo.
- Be guided by the LifeSet logic model and measure all relevant outcomes that may be affected by the intervention, especially those that can produce public savings and private benefits.
- Capture the associated magnitude (or quantity) of the impacts to go beyond simply measuring the incidence of any given outcome. For example, for homelessness, measure the number of nights and type of homelessness for each episode (e.g., staying with a friend, staying in a shelter). For public benefits, measure the months of receipt of cash and in-kind transfers and the number of times economic hardship was experienced (e.g., the number of months when bills were not paid). For human capital investments, such as postsecondary education and training programs, measure the number of credits earned or credentials received. Capturing these outcomes in more depth would support more-precise estimation of the economic value of the impacts of LifeSet.
- Extend the measurement of outcomes beyond the end of the intervention to capture longer-term impacts. Ideally, these would consist of measures of human capital

---

those with the greatest risk profile. See Karoly et al. (1998) and Karoly, Kilburn, and Cannon (2005) for illustrations.

acquisition, such as certificates or degrees conferred, and outcomes related to labor market performance, health status and health care utilization, social welfare program use, economic hardship, criminal involvement, and so on. Reliance on administrative data for earning histories, postsecondary education outcomes, and criminal justice system involvement can support longer-term measurement, but it is also important to survey treatment and control group members periodically to measure longer-term outcomes that are not captured by administrative data.

Youth Villages has demonstrated a commitment to evaluating the impacts of LifeSet and its other programs serving children and young adults in the child welfare system. The addition of economic evaluation—cost analysis, cost-effectiveness analysis, and BCA—further strengthens the understanding of the resources required for program implementation, as well as the potential for economic benefits for program participants and the rest of the society (as taxpayers and as private citizens) to outweigh the program costs.

Appendix A. Methods and Findings from the WSIPP BCA of LifeSet

With a mandate from the Washington state legislature, WSIPP has developed a sophisticated BCA model for analyzing the costs and benefits of an array of social programs across several human services sectors (WSIPP, 2018b). WSIPP generates dollar estimates specific to Washington state, both in estimating the cost to implement a given program in the state and in the estimated value of the outcomes produced by the program. Therefore, the WSIPP model provides prospective BCAs for the programs analyzed, one of which is LifeSet.

This appendix provides a summary of the methods and findings from the WSIPP BCA model for LifeSet. This discussion is based on estimates for LifeSet updated by WSIPP in December 2018 (WSIPP, 2018a). Before we review the BCA findings, we discuss the following BCA components: program cost, program impacts, and valuation of program impacts and other assumptions.

WSIPP Estimate of LifeSet Program Cost in Washington State

The WSIPP model derives a per-participant cost estimate for LifeSet of $9,690 in 2015 dollars. This comes from assuming an average daily cost of $40 to $50 and an enrollment duration for the average young adult of 215 days, based on information provided to WSIPP by Youth Villages. The midpoint of the daily cost, $45, is used for the estimate. When discounted and converted to 2016 dollars, the per-participant cost estimate for LifeSet in Washington in the WSIPP model is $9,802. This estimate is below the $11,841 estimate for the Tennessee evaluation. This may reflect somewhat lower staff salaries and other input costs in Washington state compared with Tennessee.

The WSIPP calculations do not account for the costs of the services received on the part of the control group (status quo). Hence, the cost estimate is likely an overestimate of the incremental cost to deliver LifeSet, after accounting for the usual services that would have occurred in the absence of LifeSet. Because the WSIPP BCA is based on the impacts of LifeSet as measured in the MDRC evaluation (Valentine, Skemer, and Courtney, 2015), in which the control group received some services, the costs of LifeSet should likewise be measured relative to a status quo with some service use.

WSIPP Estimates of LifeSet Program Impacts

The WSIPP model estimates impacts using evaluations of the program being analyzed and incorporates a wide array of potential impacts from social programs. However, as a general model, it is not designed to capture all possible impacts from social programs. In other words, it does not conduct a tailored BCA for each program, with the goal of valuing all possible domains of impact. Impacts from a program in domains not captured by the WSIPP BCA will therefore be omitted. This may lead to an underestimate or overestimate of net benefits and the benefit-cost ratio, depending on whether the omitted impacts would lead to additional benefits or costs, on net.

Omitted Domains of Impact

In the case of LifeSet, the WSIPP impact estimates are based on the MDRC evaluation that measured effects one year after randomization (Valentine, Skemer, and Courtney, 2015). The December 2018 WSIPP model does not incorporate findings from the LifeSet evaluation year 2 follow-up (Skemer and Valentine, 2016). As noted in Chapter 2, the second year of follow-up includes impacts for educational enrollment, employment, earnings, and crime, based on administrative data. This means that the WSIPP BCA result for LifeSet does not account for the set of favorable and unfavorable impacts in the second year after the start of the intervention. The overall effect on net benefits from this omission is unclear.

Even for the year 1 findings, the WSIPP model does not account for all of the outcomes measured in the MDRC evaluation. In particular, as shown in Table A.1, the WSIPP model accounts for just five specific impacts measured in the LifeSet evaluation: high school graduation, employment, earnings, problem alcohol use, and crime.[9] The WSIPP model does not account for the following statistically significant impacts observed in the MDRC evaluation: the reduction in housing instability (such as homelessness and couch-surfing), the reduction in economic hardship, the increased use of SNAP benefits, the reduction in mental health problems, the reduction in partner violence, and the reduction in criminal behavior (specifically, receiving cash or goods in exchange for sex). These outcomes would generally be expected to produce benefits for participants themselves and, in most cases, benefits to taxpayers because of reduced public-sector costs. The one exception is the increase in SNAP benefits, which would increase transfer payments paid by taxpayers. However, viewed from the perspective of society as a whole, the cost to taxpayers is offset by the benefit to LifeSet participants. (Any administrative costs for the program do result in a net cost to society when transfer payments increase.)

---

[9] The WSIPP model also shows an estimate of the effect size for homelessness, but that outcome was not monetized as of the December 2018 version of the model.

Table A.1. LifeSet Impacts in MDRC Evaluation and Those Included in WSIPP BCA

Outcome	Impacts in MDRC Evaluation	Included in WSIPP BCA	Projected in WSIPP BCA
Education and training			
Attainment (diploma/GED)	Year 1	Yes	No
Participated in vocational training	Year 1		
Enrolled in postsecondary education*	Year 1, year 2		
Employment and earnings			
Earnings (self-reported, UI records)	Year 1, year 2	Yes	No
Employment rate (self-reported, UI records)*	Year 1, year 2	Yes	No
Housing stability and economic well-being			
Housing instability (homelessness, couch-surfing)	Year 1		
Economic hardship	Year 1		
Savings*	Year 1		
Debt*	Year 1		
Received SSI*	Year 1		
Received SNAP*	Year 1		
Received WIC*	Year 1		
Received public housing/rental assistance*	Year 1		
Received Families First (TANF)*	Year 1		
Health and safety			
Mental health problems	Year 1		
Self-reported general health*	Year 1		
Had a regular source of care*	Year 1		
Received a physical exam, dental exam*	Year 1		
Did not receive care when needed*	Year 1		
Had health insurance coverage*	Year 1		
Binge drinking in past month	Year 1	Yes	Future health
Used illegal drugs	Year 1		
Condom use during last sexual encounter	Year 1		
Was robbed or assaulted	Year 1		
Partner violence	Year 1		
Social support			
Social support	Year 1		
Closeness/contact with caring adult	Year 1		
Score on familial closeness scale*	Year 1		
Biological family member would offer place to stay*	Year 1		
Friends would offer place to stay*	Year 1		
Criminal involvement			
Criminal behavior scale	Year 1		
Got in gang fight or assault*	Year 1		
Committed property crime*	Year 1		
Carried a handgun*	Year 1		
Sold or helped sell illegal drugs*	Year 1		
Received cash/goods in exchange for sex*	Year 1		
Spent 1 or more nights in jail/prison	Year 1		
Arrested	Year 1, Year 2		
Convictions (overall, by type)	Year 1, Year 2	Yes	Future crime

SOURCES: Table 2.1 (which explains this table's colors, shading, and asterisks); WSIPP, 2018a.

To be consistent with recommended practice, the WSIPP model includes categories of impacts that it is designed to value regardless of their statistical significance, and the model accounts for the uncertainty associated with each impact estimate using Monte Carlo simulation. Thus, the WSIPP model excludes from valuation the following LifeSet outcomes that are not statistically significant but favorable: participation in vocational training; debt; health status, health care utilization, and health insurance coverage; drug use; social support; and some types of criminal behavior, arrests, and jail time. To be balanced, statistically insignificant impacts that are unfavorable should be included as well, where valuation is possible. In the case of LifeSet, these outcomes include postsecondary education enrollment, savings, receipt of other government benefits, and certain types of criminal behavior. Many of these impacts are small in magnitude, in addition to not being statistically significant. Nevertheless, a comprehensive assessment of the costs and benefits of LifeSet would ideally include as many of the outcomes listed in Table A.1 as possible.

Impacts for Included Outcomes

For outcomes that are included, the WSIPP model typically generates impact estimates, measured as effect sizes and based on meta-analyses that combine the estimates from multiple studies of a given program or intervention. In the case of LifeSet, because only one set of results was used from the 12-month follow-up data, no meta-analysis was required.

WSIPP makes further adjustments to the estimated effect sizes to account for aspects of the evaluation methodology. For example, WSIPP will reduce effect sizes for small-scale evaluations (e.g., of a demonstration or pilot program) and evaluations conducted by researchers who may have an interest in the findings (i.e., not independent) or to take into account the rigor of the evaluation design. In the case of LifeSet, no such deductions are taken, because the evaluation was for a program implemented at scale (the state of Tennessee), was conducted by an independent organization, and used the gold-standard design, an RCT. Thus, the WSIPP-adjusted effect sizes are the same as the unadjusted effect sizes.

The WSIPP model also allows for effect sizes to change over time, based on either a longitudinal follow-up of impacts or other evidence of how effect sizes change over time. The WSIPP documentation thus reports an initial adjusted effect size, based on the meta-analysis, and an extended adjusted effect size, which is intended to apply to outcomes two to three years after the intervention. When insufficient information is available about longer-term impacts, the extended effect size is assumed to decay to zero.

Table A.2 shows the effect sizes deployed in the December 2018 WSIPP BCA for LifeSet. For each of the five outcomes included in the WSIPP BCA, we show the unadjusted effect size reported by WSIPP, the initial adjusted effect size, the extended adjusted effect size, and the effect size reported by MDRC. As noted, WSIPP took no deductions; thus, the initial adjusted effect size is always the same as the unadjusted effect size. There are some differences, however, between the assumed WSIPP and reported MDRC effect sizes that can largely be explained by differences in the method for calculating effect sizes (following the order in Table A.1):

- The WSIPP method for calculating the effect size of a dichotomous outcome (see WSIPP, 2018a, p. 15) produces an effect size for the combined education effect of a GED or a high school diploma of 0.06. This happens to be about the same effect size reported in the MDRC study (Valentine, Skemer, and Courtney, 2015) for receiving just a high school diploma (0.06). Had the WSIPP model used only the impact for receiving a high school diploma, the effect size would have been 0.08, which would translate into higher benefits. In this case, the extended effect size is assumed by the WSIPP model to be the same magnitude as the initial effect size, implying no decay in the education impact.
- For the employment impact, the WSIPP method for calculating the effect size produces a result of 0.13, also somewhat higher than the MDRC-reported effect size of 0.10. The extended effect size is assumed to fall to zero, implying no persistent effect on employment.
- The earnings impact is calculated by WSIPP as the percentage difference between treatment and control group earnings (17.5 percent, or 0.175), as compared with the 0.12 effect size reported by MDRC. Like the employment effect, this effect size is also assumed to decay to zero.
- The WSIPP model's effect size for the impact on the measure of alcohol use is approximately the same as the one reported by MDRC and is assumed to persist, but with a diminished impact.
- The WSIPP model uses convictions as the crime indicator, which showed an increase in the MDRC evaluation, with a reported effect size of 0.07. The WSIPP methodology produces a somewhat higher effect size of 0.104. And the effect is assumed to persist. Had the result for arrests been used instead, the impact would have been negative (a favorable outcome), with an effect size of –0.040, as reported by MDRC. This also would have produced higher net benefits.

Table A.2. WSIPP Effect Sizes Versus MDRC Evaluation

Outcome	Follow-Up Interval	WSIPP Unadjusted Effect Size	WSIPP Initial Adjusted Effect Size	WSIPP Extended Adjusted Effect Size	MDRC-Reported Effect Size
High school graduation	Year 1	0.056	0.056	0.056	0.06
Any employment	Year 1	0.133	0.133	0.000	0.10
Earnings	Year 1	0.175	0.175	0.000	0.12
Problem alcohol use	Year 1	–0.079	–0.079	–0.011	–0.07
Crime (convictions)	Year 1	0.104	0.104	0.104	0.07

SOURCES: WSIPP, 2018a; Valentine, Skemer, and Courtney, 2015.

The bottom line is that, when the same outcome measure is used, the WSIPP model employs somewhat larger estimates of effect size than those reported in the MDRC evaluation because of a difference in the method used for effect size calculations. This has the effect of raising the monetary benefits associated with favorable outcomes but also raising the costs when impacts are unfavorable. At the same time, when there are choices about which specific outcome indicators to use, the WSIPP methodology happens to choose indicators in the education attainment and crime domains that produce lower net benefit estimates.

WSIPP Valuation of Program Impacts and Other BCA Model Assumptions

For each of the specific impacts listed in Table A.2, the WSIPP model has assumptions that produce an economic value associated with that outcome. These valuations apply to observed impacts; where effect sizes are nonzero for extended impacts, the valuations apply in the longer run as well. These valuations are specific to Washington state, whenever possible. Because costs are also specific to the state, the ratio of benefits to cost may be a fairly reliable estimate for what might result in another state, assuming that the costs of all inputs and value of outcomes in that state differ from Washington state in a constant proportion (i.e., a regional price deflator). This assumption might not be valid where there are important institutional differences across states, such as the cost of the criminal justice system or the generosity of social welfare programs.

The WSIPP model has several other assumptions required for implementing a BCA. For the most part, these are standard assumptions, consistent with recommendations for best practices, such as those delineated by the National Academy of Sciences (Steurle and Jackson, 2016). These include assumptions about the discount rate (assumed to be 3.5 percent as the modal value but ranging from 2 to 5 percent) and the use of Monte Carlo simulation to account for the uncertainty in the BCA model parameters.

Another key assumption in the WSIPP model is the inclusion of a parameter to capture the efficiency cost of raising taxes to pay for government transfers and other benefits, known as *deadweight loss*. In effect, every dollar of public revenue required to pay for the direct program costs or any unintended consequences is assumed to cost more than a dollar because of unintended behavior change (e.g., reduced work effort) caused by tax-raising mechanisms. Alternatively, when there are government savings, there will be the additional benefit of the avoidance of deadweight loss, because those tax revenues do not need to be raised. In its simulations, WSIPP assumes a distribution for the deadweight-loss parameter from 0 to 100 and a modal value of 50. A value of 50 means that it costs $1.50 to raise $1 of revenue. Some would argue that the modal value used by WSIPP might be on the high side, but it is well within in the range of what is used in other BCA analyses.

WSIPP BCA Findings

Table A.3 summarizes the results of the WSIPP BCA, showing the present-value costs and benefits (in 2017 dollars) in total and disaggregated by three key stakeholders: program participants, taxpayers, and other members of society who did not participate in the program. Indirect benefits are shown in a separate column, which includes the deadweight-loss estimate. With the exception of the benefits of greater labor market earnings and the small benefits attributable to reduced problem alcohol use, all of the other impacts generate costs. The bottom line is an estimated present-value net benefit of LifeSet of just over –$13,000 per participant—in other words, a negative bottom line.

As discussed in the body of the report, this estimate differs from the results presented in Chapter 4 in important ways:

- The WSIPP analysis is prospective and based on a limited set of the outcomes affected by LifeSet and then uses only the first-year impact estimates.
- The estimate of the cost of LifeSet for the BCA should account for the services used by the control group, which the WSIPP analysis does not do. This has the effect of raising the marginal cost of LifeSet and thereby decreasing the estimated net benefits, all else equal.

A tailored BCA for LifeSet can value as many domains of impact as possible, both outcome domains that may provide positive dollar benefits and some domains that may produce unintended adverse outcomes with dollar costs. Thus, all else equal, the valuation of more outcomes may increase or decrease the total estimated net benefits (or benefit-cost ratio) for LifeSet.

Table A.3. WSIPP Model BCA Results

	By Stakeholder Group				
Summary Result	**Participants**	**Taxpayers**	**Rest of Society**	**Indirect**	**Society Total**
Present-value costs, in 2017 dollars	0	–9,963	0	0	–9,963
Present-value benefits, in 2017 dollars	3,466	816	–2,017	–5,328	–3,063
Labor market earnings from employment	3,461	1,572	0	0	5,033
Problem alcohol use, property loss	1	0	2	0	3
Problem alcohol use, health care cost	4	24	26	12	66
Problem alcohol use, mortality cost	0	0	0	9	9
Crime benefits	0	–780	–2,044	–87	–3,211
Deadweight cost, in 2017 dollars	0	0	0	–4,962	–4,962
Present-value net benefits, in 2017 dollars	3,466	–9,147	–2,017	–5,328	–13,026

SOURCE: WSIPP, 2018a.
NOTES: The indirect benefits include the deadweight-loss estimate and changes in the value of a statistical life.

Appendix B. Impact Estimates from Evaluation of LifeSet

The tables in this appendix catalog the set of findings reported in the two MDRC evaluation reports of LifeSet (Valentine, Skemer, and Courtney, 2015; Skemer and Valentine, 2016). The tables cover outcomes in the following domains: education and training (Table B.1), employment and earnings (Table B.2), housing stability (Table B.3), economic well-being (Table B.4), health (Table B.5), safety (Table B.6), social support (Table B.7), and criminal involvement (Table B.8).[10]

Each table shows the outcome indicator, the source of data (the 12-month survey or a source of administrative data), the mean outcome for the control group, the impact estimate (treatment-control difference), the corresponding effect size (when reported), and the *p*-value of the impact estimate. (The mean outcome for the treatment group is the sum of the impact estimate and the control group mean.)

Table B.1. One- and Two-Year Impact Estimates: Education and Training

Outcome	Source	Control Group	Impact (T – C)	Effect Size	*p*-value
Educational attainment					
Year 1: Has high school diploma (%)	12-mo. survey	52.5	3.2	0.06	0.233
Year 1: Has GED certificate (%)	12-mo. survey	17.2	–1.3	–0.03	0.571
Training					
Year 1: Participated in vocational training (%)	12-mo. survey	8.9	2.8	0.10	0.139
Postsecondary educational enrollment*					
Years 1–2: Enrolled (%)	NSC data	25.4	–3.4	—	0.111
Year 1: Enrolled (%)	NSC data	18.4	0.4	0.01	0.821
Year 2: Enrolled (%)	NSC data	13.6	–2.2	—	0.212
Year 1: Institution type where enrolled*					
Enrolled in 4-year college (%)	NSC data	7.5	–0.4	–0.02	0.771
Enrolled in 2-year college (%)	NSC data	11.3	1.6	0.05	0.341
Years 1–2: Institution type where enrolled*					
Enrolled in 4-year college (%)	NSC data	10.3	–2.2	—	0.154
Enrolled in 2-year college (%)	NSC data	16.8	–1.1	—	0.595

SOURCES: Valentine, Skemer, and Courtney, 2015, Table 5.1; Skemer and Valentine, 2016, Table 3.
NOTES: — = not reported. Asterisks denote secondary outcomes. Year 1 sample sizes for the 12-month survey are treatment (T) = 659 and control (C) = 455. Year 1 and year 2 sample sizes for the NSC administrative data are T = 788, C = 534.

[10] For ease of presentation, the outcomes in the housing stability and economic well-being domain are divided into two tables, and outcomes in the health and safety domain are also reported in two tables.

Table B.2. One- and Two-Year Impact Estimates: Employment and Earnings

Outcome	Source	Control Group	Impact (T – C)	Effect Size	*p*-value
Earnings from formal work—year 1, year 2					
Earnings—year 1 ($)	12-mo. survey	3,488	611	0.12	0.043
Earnings—years 1–2 ($)	UI data	5,016	224	—	0.555
Earnings—year 1 ($)	UI data	2,130	103	—	0.562
Earnings are $2,500 or more (%)	UI data	25.5	5.1	—	0.035
Earnings are $5,000 or more (%)	UI data	13.4	3.3	—	0.083
Earnings are $7,500 or more (%)	UI data	7.9	1.1	—	0.462
Earnings—year 2 ($)	UI data	2,885	121	—	0.641
Earnings are $2,500 or more (%)	UI data	30.3	6.3	—	0.016
Earnings are $5,000 or more (%)	UI data	19.2	3.7	—	0.105
Earnings are $7,500 or more (%)	UI data	13.1	1.1	—	0.566
Ever employed*—year 1, year 2					
Any employment—year 1 (%)	12-mo. survey	65.3	4.8	0.10	0.084
Full-time employment—year 1 (%)	12-mo. survey	46.5	0.5	0.01	0.880
Part-time employment—year 1 (%)	12-mo. survey	18.4	4.6	0.12	0.068
Any employment—years 1–2 (%)	UI data	75.6	2.9	—	0.212
Any employment—year 1 (%)	UI data	59.3	4.8	—	0.072
Any employment—year 2 (%)	UI data	60.0	3.5	—	0.566
Quarters employed*—year 1, year 2 (*N*)	UI data	3.0	0.2	—	0.088

SOURCES: Valentine, Skemer, and Courtney, 2015, Table 5.2; Skemer and Valentine, 2016, Table 4.
NOTES: — = not reported. Asterisks denote secondary outcomes. Year 1 sample sizes for the 12-month survey are T = 659, C = 455. Year 1 and year 2 sample sizes for the UI administrative data are T = 788, C = 534.

Table B.3. One-Year Impact Estimates: Housing Stability

Outcome	Source	Control Group	Impact (T – C)	Effect Size	*p*-value
Score on housing stability scale (range: 0–4)	12-mo. survey	1.2	–0.2	–0.16	0.005
Experienced homelessness* (%)	12-mo. survey	27.2	–6.1	–0.14	0.017
Couch-surfed* (%)	12-mo. survey	44.1	–8.4	–0.17	0.005
Was unable to pay rent* (%)	12-mo. survey	30.0	–4.0	–0.09	0.146
Lost housing because unable to pay rent* (%)	12-mo. survey	18.3	–2.8	–0.09	0.224

SOURCE: Valentine, Skemer, and Courtney, 2015, Table 6.1.
NOTES: Asterisks denote secondary outcomes. Year 1 sample sizes for the 12-month survey are T = 659, C = 455.

Table B.4. One-Year Impact Estimates: Economic Well-Being

Outcome	Source	Control Group	Impact (T – C)	Effect Size	*p*-value
Score on economic hardship scale (range: 0–5)	12-mo. survey	1.5	–0.2	–0.13	0.022
Did not have necessary clothing/shoes* (%)	12-mo. survey	33.4	–6.3	–0.13	0.024
Was unable to pay utility bill* (%)	12-mo. survey	24.0	–2.3	–0.05	0.381
Gas/electricity shut off because unable to pay* (%)	12-mo. survey	15.1	–2.3	–0.07	0.272
Phone service shut off because unable to pay* (%)	12-mo. survey	48.1	–3.6	–0.07	0.231
Delayed paying a bill to buy food* (%)	12-mo. survey	27.8	–6.2	–0.14	0.019
Savings* ($)	12-mo. survey	318	–120	–0.06	0.264
Debt* ($)	12-mo. survey	1,492	–429	–0.09	0.109
Receipt of public benefits					
Received SSI* (%)	12-mo. survey	6.9	2.0	0.08	0.230
Received SNAP* (%)	12-mo. survey	51.4	6.1	0.12	0.036
Received WIC* (%)	12-mo. survey	16.2	0.8	0.02	0.710
Received public housing/rental assistance* (%)	12-mo. survey	7.1	1.6	0.06	0.337
Received Families First (TANF)* (%)	12-mo. survey	8.6	–0.8	–0.03	0.631

SOURCE: Valentine, Skemer, and Courtney, 2015, Table 6.1.
NOTES: Asterisks denote secondary outcomes. Year 1 sample sizes for the 12-month survey are T = 659, C = 455.

Table B.5. One-Year Impact Estimates: Health

Outcome	Source	Control Group	Impact (T – C)	Effect Size	*p*-value
Score on mental health problem scale (range: 0–63)	12-mo. survey	11.2	–1.4	–0.13	0.025
Self-reported general health* (%)	12-mo. survey				0.104
Excellent/very good		65.0	3.6	0.08	
Good		21.2	0.6	0.02	
Fair/poor		13.8	–4.2	–0.12	
Had a regular source of care* (%)	12-mo. survey	59.5	3.9	0.08	0.193
Received a physical exam* (%)	12-mo. survey	58.0	4.3	0.09	0.147
Received a dental exam* (%)	12-mo. survey	53.3	4.0	0.08	0.186
Did not receive care when needed* (%)	12-mo. survey	36.2	–6.8	–0.14	0.018
Had health insurance coverage* (%)	12-mo. survey	76.5	3.1	0.07	0.228

SOURCE: Valentine, Skemer, and Courtney, 2015, Table 8.1.
NOTES: Asterisks denote secondary outcomes. Year 1 sample sizes for the 12-month survey are T = 659, C = 455.

Table B.6. One-Year Impact Estimates: Safety

Outcome	Source	Control Group	Impact (T – C)	Effect Size	*p*-value
Substance use					
Days of binge drinking in past month (*N*)	12-mo. survey	0.9	–0.2	–0.07	0.197
Used illegal drugs (%)	12-mo. survey	32.8	–1.4	–0.03	0.622
Used a condom during last sexual encounter (%)	12-mo. survey				0.360
Yes		47.7	1.8	0.04	
No		40.3	–3.7	–0.08	
Not sexually active		12.0	1.9	0.06	
Was robbed or assaulted (%)	12-mo. survey	24.2	0.2	0.01	0.929
Partner violence (%)	12-mo. survey				0.021
In a violent relationship		21.5	–6.4	–0.16	
In a nonviolent relationship		36.3	2.3	0.05	
Not in a relationship		42.2	4.1	0.08	

SOURCE: Valentine, Skemer, and Courtney, 2015, Table 8.2.
NOTES: Asterisks denote secondary outcomes. Year 1 sample sizes for the 12-month survey are T = 659, C = 455.

Table B.7. One-Year Impact Estimates: Social Support

Outcome	Source	Control Group	Impact (T – C)	Effect Size	*p*-value
Score on social support scale (range: 0–99)	12-mo. survey	4.2	0.2	0.05	0.421
Very close to an adult (%)	12-mo. survey	91.2	0.8	0.03	0.639
Frequency of contact with caring adult* (%)	12-mo. survey				0.655
Did not report a caring adult		10.2	–0.6	–0.02	
Less than once a month		5.4	–1.6	–0.07	
Between once a month and once a week		16.6	0.7	0.02	
Several times a week to almost every day		67.8	1.5	0.03	
Frequency of in-person contact with caring adult* (%)	12-mo. survey				0.644
Did not report a caring adult		10.2	–0.6	–0.02	
Less than once a month		13.2	–1.1	–0.03	
Between once a month and once a week		22.4	3.3	0.08	
Several times a week to almost every day		54.2	–1.6	–0.03	
Score on familial closeness scale (range: 0–18)*	12-mo. survey	7.9	0.1	0.01	0.801
Biological family member would offer respondent a place to stay if needed* (%)	12-mo. survey				0.497
Not at all likely		16.1	2.6	0.07	
Somewhat likely		30.8	–3.4	–0.07	
Very likely		16.8	1.4	0.04	
Definitely		36.3	–0.7	–0.01	
Friends would offer respondent a place to stay if needed* (%)	12-mo. survey				0.325
Not at all likely		12.4	–2.3	–0.07	
Somewhat likely		33.8	–2.2	–0.05	
Very likely		26.3	4.4	0.10	
Definitely		27.5	0.1	0.00	

SOURCE: Valentine, Skemer, and Courtney, 2015, Table 7.1.
NOTES: Asterisks denote secondary outcomes. Year 1 sample sizes for the 12-month survey are T = 659, C = 455.

Table B.8. One- and Two-Year Impact Estimates: Criminal Involvement

Outcome	Source	Control Group	Impact (T – C)	Effect Size	*p*-value
Criminal behavior—year 1					
Score on criminal behavior scale (range: 0–10)	12-mo. survey	0.6	0.0	0.03	0.664
Types of crime committed*—year 1					
Gang fight or assault (%)	12-mo. survey	13.1	0.5	0.02	0.805
Property crime (%)	12-mo. survey	17.2	–1.4	–0.04	0.544
Carried a handgun (%)	12-mo. survey	7.9	1.2	0.04	0.490
Sold or helped sell illegal drugs (%)	12-mo. survey	7.0	2.2	0.09	0.203
Received cash/goods in exchange for sex (%)	12-mo. survey	4.3	–2.2	–0.11	0.044
Time in jail/prison—year 1					
Spent 1+ nights in jail/prison (%)	12-mo. survey	25.2	–2.1	–0.05	0.405
Arrests—year 1, year 2					
Arrested–year 1 (%)	12-mo. survey	25.9	–1.5	–0.04	0.549
Arrested–years 1–2 (%)	TBI data	47.6	0.1	—	0.972
Arrested–year 1 (%)	TBI data	31.1	–0.4	—	0.877
Arrested–year 2 (%)	TBI data	34.9	–0.9	—	0.721
Convictions—year 1, year 2					
Convicted of a crime—year 1 (%)	12-mo. survey	14.8	2.3	0.07	0.301
Convicted of a crime—years 1–2 (%)	TBI data	17.7	2.0	—	0.350
Convicted of a crime—year 1 (%)	TBI data	9.5	1.0	—	0.564
Convicted of a crime—year 2 (%)	TBI data	12.6	0.9	—	0.635
Class of conviction*—years 1–2					
Felony (%)	TBI data	5.3	1.1	—	0.398
Misdemeanor (%)	TBI data	15.3	0.4	—	0.861
Category of conviction*—years 1–2					
Violent crime (%)	TBI data	3.0	1.4	—	0.189
Property crime (%)	TBI data	5.7	2.0	—	0.167
Drug crime (%)	TBI data	4.7	–0.2	—	0.858
Public-order crime (%)	TBI data	9.9	–0.1	—	0.966

SOURCES: Valentine, Skemer, and Courtney, 2015, Table 8.3; Skemer and Valentine, 2016, Table 5.
NOTES: — = not reported. TBI = Tennessee Bureau of Investigation. Asterisks denote secondary outcomes. Year 1 sample sizes for the 12-month survey are T = 659, C = 455. Year 1 and year 2 sample sizes for the TBI administrative data are T = 788, C = 534.

Appendix C. Adjustment to Program Cost

This appendix provides additional documentation of how we derived our estimate of the value of the services and support received by the control group.

As noted in Chapter 5, the MDRC evaluation (Skemer and Valentine, 2016) estimated that the cost of delivering the LifeSet program was $11,841 per participant in 2015 dollars (see Table C.1). These costs consist of staff salaries and benefits, Youth Villages overhead, travel, operations and maintenance, and direct support to youth.

Table C.1. LifeSet Cost per Participant

Cost Category	Cost (2015 $)
Staff salaries and benefits	8,952
Service providers	7,082
Administrative staff	1,869
Corporate overhead	1,137
Travel	1,088
Operations and maintenance	396
Direct support to youth	269
Total	11,841

SOURCE: Skemer and Valentine, 2016, Table 6.
NOTE: Cost components might not sum to totals because of rounding.

Information on the cost of the services used by the control group was not collected. Instead, we use information from the 12-month survey of treatment and control group members to estimate those costs (Valentine, Skemer, and Courtney, 2015). In particular, in the first step, we use information for the treatment group about the hours spent with the LifeSet specialist and compute a cost per hour based on the salaries and benefits for LifeSet service providers and for administrative staff. In the second step, we apply this hourly rate to the estimated hours of contact with a caseworker for the control group participants. Note that the costs for LifeSet also consist of corporate overhead, travel, operations and maintenance, and direct support to youth (see Table C.1). We have not included these cost categories for the control group, assuming that the services received are less intensive (and therefore less costly) than those received by the treatment group. This is likely to be a conservative assumption, which means that we would understate the value of the resources used by the control group and therefore overstate the net cost of LifeSet beyond the status quo.

Caseworker Contact Hours for Treatment and Control Group Members

According to the 12-month survey data reported in Valentine, Skemer, and Courtney (2015), 75 percent of the treatment group and 44 percent of the control group reported receiving help from a case manager (see Table C.2), defined as a social worker, case manager, caseworker, or LifeSet specialist. Just over 60 percent of the LifeSet group had at least weekly contact, compared with the control group, in which contact was less frequent. The survey data also show that the two groups received similar types of assistance, albeit with less frequency for the control group. Given the level of service use on the part of the control group, it is important to account for that service use when constructing the cost estimate of LifeSet relative to the control group experience.

Table C.2. Service Utilization by Treatment and Control Group Participants

Indicator	Source	Treatment Group	Control Group
Received help from a case manager (%)	12-mo. survey	74.5	44.2
Frequency of contact with case manager (%)	12-mo. survey		
More than once per week		21.9	8.2
Once per week		38.5	12.1
More than once per month		4.6	6.2
About once per month		6.7	10.4
Less than once per month		2.5	6.5
Did not have a case manager		25.7	56.5
Received help preparing for future education (%)	12-mo. survey	49.9	36.6
Received help obtaining employment (%)	12-mo. survey	62.5	40.7
Received help handling finances (%)	12-mo. survey	60.4	38.6
Received help obtaining housing (%)	12-mo. survey	33.8	19.6
Received help developing life skills (%)	12-mo. survey	51.0	36.6

SOURCE: Valentine, Skemer, and Courtney, 2015, Table 4.1.
NOTES: Year 1 sample sizes for the 12-month survey are T = 659, C = 455.

We use the frequency-of-contact information to estimate the number of contacts, on average, for treatment and control group members. We assume the following numbers of visits associated with the categories in Table C.2:

- those with contact more than once per week had 1.3 visits per week, or about 67 visits over a 52-week year
- those with contact once per week had 52 visits per year
- those with contact more than once per month had an average of 2 visits per month, or 24 visits per year
- those with a visit once per month had 12 visits per year
- those with a visit less than once per month had 6 visits per year.

With those assumptions and the distribution of participants by the number of visits, we estimate that the treatment group had an average of 36.9 contacts with a case manager over the year, and the control group had an average of 15 contacts in the 12-month period.

The estimate for the treatment group accords with other information captured in the Youth Villages management information system, specifically for the LifeSet participants. In particular, participants attended 26 regular sessions, on average, which lasted 75 minutes, on average (see Table C.3). In addition, there were communications outside the regular sessions, either lasting less than 15 minutes (about 9 sessions, on average) or more than 15 minutes (about 1 session, on average). On average, another 1.4 sessions were of unknown duration. This results in a total number of sessions and other contacts of 37.3, on average, very close to the estimate based on the reported frequency of contact by participants of about 36.9.

Table C.3. Participation in LifeSet Sessions for Treatment Group Participants

Indicator	Average Number of Sessions	Average Minutes per Session	Assumed Minutes per Session
LifeSet regular sessions with specialist	26.1	75	75
LifeSet short contacts with specialist	8.8	<15	10
LifeSet long contacts with specialist	1.0	>15	20
LifeSet contacts with specialist of unknown duration	1.4	—	—
Total number of sessions	37.3	—	—

SOURCE: Valentine, Skemer, and Courtney, 2015, Table 3.1.
NOTES: Year 1 sample size for the management information system data is T = 788. — = not applicable.

Based on assuming 75, 10, and 20 minutes, on average, for the regular sessions, short contacts, and long contacts, respectively, each LifeSet participant is estimated to have had 34.4 hours of contact with their specialists, meaning that each contact, on average, was approximately one hour. Given our estimate of 15 contacts, on average, for control group participants, we assume that those sessions were also one hour, on average. Thus, we estimate about 15 hours of contact with a case manager for control group members.

Hourly Cost for Case Worker Contact

The final step is to estimate the cost per hour of contact with a case manager for LifeSet. As noted, to be conservative, we focus only on the staff salaries and benefits of the overall cost of LifeSet. With our estimate of 34.4 hours and cost for service provider salaries per participant of $7,082, we have an estimate of $206 per hour of contact ($7,082 divided by 34.4). Adding in the administrative staff, the cost per hour of contact is about $260 ($8,952 for staff salaries and benefits divided by 34.4). Applying these two estimates of hourly cost to the 15 hours of contact estimated for the control group, on average, results in cost estimates for control group services ranging from $3,078 per participant (more precisely, 14.96 hours times $205.72 per hour) to

$3,890 (14.96 hours times $260.02 per hour). These two figures are the cost offsets recorded in Table 4.1.

Appendix D. Monte Carlo Simulation Analysis

There are multiple sources of uncertainty when conducting a BCA. These include the estimates of program cost, the estimated causal impacts of the program on the measured outcomes, and the economic values assigned to the impacts. In the case of LifeSet, for example, we have uncertainty in the value of the resources used by youth in the control group (see Appendix C), which means that there is uncertainty in our estimate of net program cost (the cost of LifeSet compared with the status quo). To capture the benefits from participating in LifeSet, we relied on estimates of causal impact from the MDRC experimental evaluation (see Valentine, Skemer, and Courtney, 2015; Skemer and Valentine, 2016). Those impact parameters (documented in the tables in Appendix B) all have a point estimate and a standard error. Some parameters are more precisely estimated—i.e., with a narrow confidence interval—than others. Finally, as discussed in Chapter 3, there is also uncertainty in the economic values that we use to convert program impacts into dollar values that can be aggregated and compared with program costs.

In Chapter 4, in recognition of the uncertainty in conducting the BCA, we presented results using more conservative estimates (lower bound) and less conservative estimates (upper bound). These bounds essentially reflect the range of the economic values associated with the outcomes, as well as the bounds on the estimate of program services used by the control group. (One exception was the estimated earning effect, in which the smaller estimate was taken from the two-year impact based on the administrative survey and the larger estimate was taken from the one-year impact based on self-reported data). As an alternative, we also conducted a Monte Carlo simulation analysis to account for these sources of uncertainty, as well as the uncertainty in the causal impact estimates. This approach is considered a best practice by a National Academy of Sciences panel (Steurle and Jackson, 2016), and the approach is also used in the WSIPP BCA model (WSIPP, 2018a).

For all parameters with uncertainty, the Monte Carlo analysis performs a series of random draws from an assumed distribution for each parameter used to produce the estimated per-participant present-value net benefits. For a given "trial," the resulting parameters are used to compute the estimated net benefits based on those parameters. The results from multiple trials produce a distribution of results that can be summarized in terms of the mean, median, and other distributional parameters. In our case, we performed the simulation with 5,000 draws (or trials) using the software package Crystal Ball. In addition to the mean estimate of net benefits, we also computed the percentage of the trials in which net benefits were positive, similar to the summary measure used by WSIPP.

Table D.1 shows the parameters that were varied in the Monte Carlo simulation and the distributional assumptions:

- The value of the services used by the control group assumes a uniform distribution with a minimum and maximum set to the range estimated in Appendix C.
- Impact estimates (differences between the treatment and control groups) are assumed to follow a normal distribution, based on the impact estimate and the associated standard error (see Appendix A).
- We assumed a uniform distribution for the economic values for all outcomes included in the BCA, with the same range used in the more and less conservative estimates (as reported in Chapter 3).
- For transfer programs, the benefits to society are based on the estimated administrative costs. We assumed a uniform distribution and an administrative cost rate that ranged from 10 to 20 percent (see the discussion in Chapter 3).
- The parameter for deadweight loss is assumed to follow a triangle distribution, centered on 0.25, with a minimum of 0 and a maximum of 0.50.

Table D.1. Parameter Assumptions for Monte Carlo Simulation

Indicator	Assumed Distribution	Distribution Parameters
Value of services used by the control group	Uniform	Range of $3,078 to $3,890 (Appendix C)
Impact estimates (differences between treatment and control groups)	Normal	RCT impact estimates and standard errors (Appendix A)
Economic values for outcomes with impact estimates	Uniform	Lower and upper bounds used in the more and less conservative assumptions (Chapter 3)
Administrative cost rate for transfer programs	Uniform	Range of 10% to 20%
Deadweight-loss parameter	Triangle	Minimum of 0, midpoint of 0.25, maximum of 0.50

NOTE: Standard errors for the treatment and control group impact estimates were computed based on the reported impact estimate and *p*-value.

In the case of the estimated effect of LifeSet participation on earnings, the more conservative estimate was based on the estimated (discounted) earnings gain over two years using administrative data ($225), while the less conservative estimate was based on the earnings gain measured over one year as reported in the participant survey ($631). Because each of these earnings estimates themselves had a standard error, we performed one set of simulations using the lower-bound earnings estimate and another set using the upper-bound earnings estimate. The results of the Monte Carlo simulations are reported in Table D.2, first using the lower-bound earnings estimate and second using the upper-bound earnings estimate. The two sets of results are very similar, with a mean and median that vary by about $400, the difference between the two earning impact estimates. The average result across the two simulations is approximately the same as the base case reported in Table 4.1, about $1,000 in present-value net benefits per LifeSet participant. In both simulations, present-value net benefits are positive for about 53 percent of the simulations. The 30th percentile is about the same as the more conservative estimate, while the 70th percentile is close to the less conservative estimate (see Table 4.1).

Table D.2. Monte Carlo Simulation Results

Simulation Result	Simulation Based on Lower-Bound Earning Impact	Simulation Based on Upper-Bound Earning Impact
Mean per-participant present-value net benefits (2015 $)	837	1,253
Percentile points, per-participant present-value net benefits (2015 $)		
30th percentile	–4,656	–4,605
50th percentile (median)	916	1,147
70th percentile	6,267	6,692
Percentage of trials with positive present-value net benefits	53.0	53.9

NOTES: 5,000 trials were run for each simulation.

References

Bitler, Marianne P., and Lynn A. Karoly, "Intended and Unintended Effects of the War on Poverty: What Research Tells Us and Implications for Policy," *Journal of Policy Analysis and Management*, Vol. 34, No. 3, 2015, pp. 639–696.

Carlson, Deven, Robert Haveman, Thomas Kaplan, and Barbara Wolfe, "The Benefits and Costs of the Section 8 Housing Subsidy Program: A Framework and Estimates of First-Year Effects," *Journal of Policy Analysis and Management*, Vol. 30, 2011, pp. 233–255.

Cohen, Mark A., and Alex R. Piquero, "New Evidence on the Monetary Value of Saving a High Risk Youth," *Journal of Quantitative Criminology*, Vol. 25, 2009, pp. 25–49.

Heckman, James J., John Eric Humphries, and Nicholas Mader, "The GED," in Eric A. Hanushek, Stephen J. Machin, and Ludger Woessmann, eds., *Handbook of the Economics of Education*, Vol. 3, Amsterdam: North-Holland, 2011, pp. 423–484.

Heckman, James J., and Paul A. LaFontaine, "Bias-Corrected Estimates of GED Returns," *Journal of Labor Economics*, Vol. 24, No. 3, 2006, pp. 661–700.

Karoly, Lynn A., *Valuing Benefits in Benefit-Cost Studies of Social Programs*, Santa Monica, Calif.: RAND Corporation, TR-643-MCF, 2008. As of January 14, 2020: https://www.rand.org/pubs/technical_reports/TR643.html

Karoly, Lynn A., Peter W. Greenwood, Susan S. Everingham, Jill Houbé, M. Rebecca Kilburn, C. Peter Rydell, Matthew Sanders, and James Chiesa, *Investing in Our Children: What We Know and Don't Know About the Costs and Benefits of Early Childhood Interventions*, Santa Monica, Calif.: RAND Corporation, MR-898-TCWF, 1998. As of January 14, 2020: https://www.rand.org/pubs/monograph_reports/MR898.html

Karoly, Lynn A., M. Rebecca Kilburn, and Jill S. Cannon, *Early Childhood Interventions: Proven Results, Future Promise*, Santa Monica, Calif.: RAND Corporation, MG-341-PNC, 2005. As of January 14, 2020: https://www.rand.org/pubs/monographs/MG341.html

Leuven, Edwin, and Hessel Oosterbeek, "An Alternative Approach to Estimate the Wage Returns to Private-Sector Training," *Journal of Applied Econometrics*, Vol. 23, No. 4, 2008, pp. 423–434.

Levin, Henry M., and Patrick J. McEwan, *Cost-Effectiveness Analysis: Methods and Applications*, Thousand Oaks, Calif.: Sage Publications, 2001.

Manno, Michelle, Erin Jacobs, Julianna Alson, and Melanie Skemer, *Moving into Adulthood: Implementation Findings from the Youth Villages Transitional Living Evaluation*, New York: MDRC, 2014.

Roman, John K., "How Do We Measure the Severity of Crimes? New Estimates of the Cost of Criminal Victimization," in John MacDonald, ed., *Measuring Crime and Criminality: Advances in Criminological Theory*, Vol. 17, New Brunswick, N.J.: Transaction Publishers, 2011, pp. 37–70.

Rzepka, Sylvi, "Labor Market Returns to College Education with Vocational Qualifications," *Education Economics*, Vol. 26, No. 4, 2018, pp. 411–431.

Skemer, Melanie, and Erin J. Valentine, *Striving for Independence: Two-Year Impact Findings from the Youth Villages Transitional Living Evaluation*, New York: MDRC, 2016.

Social Security Administration, "SSI Federal Payment Amounts," webpage, undated. As of January 14, 2020:
https://www.ssa.gov/oact/cola/SSIamts.html

Spellman, Brooke, Jill Khadduri, Brian Sokol, Josh Leopold, and Abt Associates Inc., *Costs Associated with First-Time Homelessness for Families and Individuals*, Washington, D.C.: U.S. Department of Housing and Urban Development, 2010.

Spoth, Richard L., Max Guyll, and Susan X. Day, "Universal Family-Focused Interventions in Alcohol-Use Disorder Prevention: Cost-Effectiveness and Cost-Benefit Analyses of Two Interventions," *Journal of Studies on Alcohol*, Vol. 63, No. 2, 2002, pp. 219–228.

Steurle, Eugene, and Leigh M. Jackson, eds., *Advancing the Power of Economic Evidence for Making Informed Investments in Children, Youth, and Families*, Washington, D.C.: National Academies Press, 2016.

Urban Institute, Welfare Rules Database, undated. As of January 21, 2020:
https://wrd.urban.org/wrd/Query/query.cfm

U.S. Census Bureau, "Current Population Survey (CPS)," webpage, undated. As of January 21, 2020:
https://www.census.gov/programs-surveys/cps.html

U.S. Department of Agriculture, Food and Nutrition Service, "FY 2015 Allotments and Deduction Information," 2015. As of January 14, 2020:
https://fns-prod.azureedge.net/sites/default/files/snap/FY15_Allot_Deduct.pdf

Valentine, Erin J., Melanie Skemer, and Mark E. Courtney, *Becoming Adults: One-Year Impact Findings from the Youth Villages Transitional Living Evaluation*, New York: MDRC, 2015.

Washington State Institute for Public Policy, "Benefit-Cost Results: Youth Villages LifeSet," webpage, December 2018a. As of May 15, 2019: http://www.wsipp.wa.gov/BenefitCost/Program/660 (webpage no longer available)

———, *Benefit-Cost Technical Documentation*, Olympia, December 2018b.

WSIPP—*See* Washington State Institute for Public Policy.

Youth Villages, "LifeSet," website, undated. As of October 30, 2019: https://www.youthvillages.org/lifeset/